A *WESTERN Horseman* BOOK

THE
BACK PAGE

The Best of Baxter Black
from Western Horseman

By Baxter Black

Edited by
Fran Devereux Smith

Photography by
Gary Gaynor, Kevin Martini-Fuller and Valerie Owen

Illustrations by
Wally Badgett, Ron Bonge, Dwayne Brech, Kevin Cordtz, Mike Craig, Ernie
Franklin, Don Gill, Mad Jack Hanks, Kris Hulse, Herb Mignery, Dr. R. M. Miller,
Gary Niblett, JP Rankin and Boots Reynolds

The Back Page

Published by
WESTERN HORSEMAN magazine
3850 North Nevada Ave.
Box 7980
Colorado Springs, CO 80933-7980
800-877-5278

www.westernhorseman.com

Design, Typography, and Production
Western Horseman
Fort Worth, Texas

Front and Back Cover Illustrations
Kevin Cordtz

Printing
Versa Press
East Peoria, Illinois

Manufactured in the United States of America

First Printing: July 2009
Second Printing: November 2012
ISBN 978-0-911647-85-3

CONTENTS

FOREWORD

It has been an honor for years to be included in the prestigious pyramid of equine publications, the *Western Horseman* magazine. It's like being associated with royalty. Even more so, because it is read by people I wish I could be for even just an hour! People who know so much about the magnificent creature that brings us all together: trainers, cowpunchers, vets, rodeo hands, jockeys, grooms, showmen, horseshoers, outfitters, and backyard horse owners.

Sometimes I feel like Forrest Gump . . . a mouse in the corner of the world of cowboys. When some good team roper or horse breeder, or cutting horse owner says he reads my column in *Western Horseman*, I say, "Thanx."

But inside I'm sayin', "I can't believe it! I have his picture on my wall!"

Working with animals keeps us humble. Every time a human meets a horse, a relationship is formed. The horse doesn't care if you've met Buster Welch, can yodel like Wylie Gustafson, or have roped with Trevor Brazile. Each horse will size you up and figger you out quicker than USTRC can cash your check!

That explains the freshness, the thrill, the challenge and the primeval bond that exists between two so independent yet interdependent species. Each horse guarantees each person at least one chance.

This collection of my columns appeared monthly in *Western Horseman* from '94 to '09. The horse, Eohippus, "on third fingernail" as Joel Nelson describes him, wends through my stories and poems like the nervous system in the tip of your finger, like hydraulic brakes in a backhoe, and like whole notes in the musical bar of a man falling off a cliff!

I got here a'horseback and that's how I'm leavin'.

If I may quote the great cowboy sage Clyde Ridgeway, "I'd walk a mile to saddle a horse to go a half a mile!"

That's good stuff, Clyde. I miss ya.

ABOUT THE AUTHOR

Cowboy poet Baxter Black is a former large animal veterinarian who practiced for 13 years in the mountain west.

He has since made a living by telling cowboys stories about themselves in his Western Horseman column, radio program, RFD TV, and on stage at ag banquets, county fairs and poetry gatherings across the country.

When asked if Baxter Black is his real name, he says, "Yes it is, because it's hard to be who you aren't!"

baxterblack.com

FOR THE ARTISTS

A special thanx to the artists who have illustrated my column in *Western Horseman*: Wally Badgett, Ron Bonge, Dwayne Brech, Mike Craig, Ernie Franklin, Don Gill, Mad Jack Hanks, Kris Hulse, Herb Mignery, Dr. R. M. Miller, Gary Niblett, JP Rankin and Boots Reynolds and double-dose, overtime pay, and an autographed picture of Pancho Villa I bought in Nogales for $5, to Kevin Cordtz.

All of these talented cowboy artists have pitched in to make me look better than I am. It apparently wore some of them out. I don't envy them their talent, though I admire it so much and consider myself lucky to be in their company.

For Kevin, who has done the majority of the illustrations since the turn of the century, my heartfelt appreciation. I know *Western Horseman* gives you hazard pay and occasionally has to hire a stunt painter to protect you from poetry shrapnel, I just hope it is enough.

thanx,
baxter black

COWBOYOSITY

'The boisterous joy of bein' a cowboy.
In a nutshell, gettin' bucked off and gettin' back on.

❝ ...when the seat hits the saddle, the rope comes tight, and the wheel comes off the wagon! It's where the action is. ❞

This is to be distinguished from the romantic side of the cowboy life, which includes sunsets, Sons of the Pioneers, and Palomino horses.

To fully grasp the underlying concept that allows cowboyosity to exist, one must have an understanding of the cowboy mentality. It is an attitude, a genetic predisposition, a way of looking at life... and you don't have to be wearing a hat and boots to have this mentality!

If cowboyosity was a volcano on the Earth's surface, then cowboy mentality would be the magma beneath it. It is best demonstrated by this little joke. Hold your hand up in front of your face and repeat after me: "Betcha can't hit my hand before I move it!"

Almost every story in this section circles around the cowboy being tested by the cow, the bull, the girl, the horse, the nitwit, the Holstein steer, the mule, the mud, the bloat, and the anvil.

Although none of these pieces are likely to be recorded by traditional western singers, they are typical examples of why cowboy poetry is funny. Admittedly, it is a sort of "gallows humor" that is often adopted to reduce stress by soldiers, surgeons, and horse show judges, but it's funny to us.

These stories are the essence of cowboyosity, when the seat hits the saddle, the rope comes tight, and the wheel comes off the wagon! It's where the action is!

> On the Edge of Common Sense   BY BAXTER BLACK, DVM

The Horse Clinician

"ARE YOU TEACHING HIM A LESSON?" she asked, eager to please,
As I tried to keep from barfing, my head between my knees.
"You hung on like a wind sock! It just tickled us to death!"
Is she serious? I'm drooling, I can't hardly catch my breath.

*"When you leaned yourself up forward
      and kissed him 'tween the ears,
The whole class just went crazy! I guess you heard the cheers!"*
That must be how I broke my nose and split my upper lip,
But I guess it looked like kissin'. *"I just love your horsemanship!"*

"The way you tame the savage beast, the techniques that yer usin'."
When my tailbone hit the cantle, I felt my sphincter loosen.

*"You reckon you could show us how you did it once again?
Be nice to get some photos."* What? To show my next of kin?
I guess there goes my living will. I'm a victim of the forces.
The way this looks, I might as well go back to shoein' horses.

*"It was really so impressive,
      the way you made him load
At full gallop, sittin' backwards, from a way on down the road."*
So, that's how I hit the trailer. Think I lost a pound of flesh.
Thank goodness it was rusty and my tetanus shot was fresh.

*"Could you show us that maneuver
      where you circled like a fan
With nothin' but your buckle touchin',
      holdin' out both hands?"*
Now where'd I put my Dramamine?
      It was here the other day.
I'm feelin' kinda woozy.
      Did Ray Hunt start out this way?

I thought it would be easy to be a horse clinician.
Now it's gonna take a miracle to explain this exhibition.
How I really was in full control, above the rising panic,
Though I looked like the propeller
      on the back of the Titanic!

"It's what I call the daisy," I modestly explained.
"It takes a master trainer to achieve what I've attained."
"You should concentrate on basics, skip the fancy stuff," I warned.
Besides, I thought, any gunsel can accidentally hook
      his buckle on the horn! 🐎

ON THE EDGE OF COMMON SENSE | BY BAXTER BLACK

Definition of a Cowboy

I've often been asked, usually by gentiles (urban people) my definition of a cowboy. I'm not sure what they expect my answer to be. Maybe someone who's strong, forthright and brave? Or a professional rodeo hand? Or a movie-star idol like John Wayne?

Although those answers do cover facets of cowboydom, they miss the heart of the job description. My definition of a cowboy is someone who can replace a uterine prolapse in a range cow in a three-section pasture with nothing but a horse and a rope.

Thinkin' that through, you can see the breadth of the skills and experience required. There are many people who can ride a horse better than a regular cowhand. Many who can outrope him. Also others who are smoother or more qualified to replace a prolapse. But not many who can do it all … by themself.

The first thing that defines a cowboy is that he's there, on the scene, on duty to herd, guard, watch, protect, serve and save the cow. Range cows are good-size critters a long way from the vet clinic. Which means if one is in trouble the lone cowboy is often the difference between life and death for her. Whether she's stuck in a mud bog, mauled by a mountain lion, hung in a tree fork, shot by an arrow, afflicted with pneumonia, attacked by screw worms or prolapsed.

To help her, first she has to be restrained. Even though they're domesticated animals — they aren't tame. They're like K-Mart employees — you can't actually walk up to one. So the cowboy must be able to approach her horseback, capture her, then hold her so he can work on her ailment. This first part of the definition involves quite a bit. Say you rope her. What do you do then? There are no corrals, no squeeze chute, no cowboy assistant, tranquilizer gun, winch or net, so you neck her to a tree or trip her then sideline or cross-tie her with a piggin' string.

Part 2: putting in the prolapse. This is no small procedure even in the antiseptic surroundings of a veterinary clinic. It's still like stuffing a smoked ham down a sink drain. It's no easier on the banks of a cottonwood creek or on the shale hillside of a winter permit.

But whether it's a prolapse, a wire around the foot, or a sick calf, the Palo Duro Canyon, the Tonto Basin or the Alvord Desert, it's still cowboy, horse and rope. The basic essentials.

I've overheard people compare the abilities of trick ropers, bronc riders, horse trainers and veterinarians to those of the *workin'-for-wages* cowboy. That he is not as accomplished at their individual skills as they are, they seem disappointed. I remind these folks that he's not a professional cowboy. He just does it for a living. 🐎

TOUGH AS LEATHER

SICK COW

DON'T FENCE ME IN

IF PROLAPSE WAS A SPORT SHE'D BE A GOLD MEDALIST.

WASH HANDS AFTER USE

JPRANKIN© 2002
"THE CARTOON COWBOY"

ON THE EDGE OF COMMON SENSE | BY BAXTER BLACK

Mules Are Peculiar

Mules are peculiar. First, they're not real. They're the equivalent of a Caterpillar body on a Volkswagon chassis, with Cadillac suspension, a Cummins diesel and lawn-mower wheels. Not to mention two dish antennae and a rear window wiper. So it's no wonder that people who are attracted to mules are peculiar in their own right.

And, just like the animals they admire, mule people are proud of their "unique-ness." I'm not sure how to characterize this condition, but I once described Bishop, Calif., Mule Days as, "like a cowboy poetry gathering, only more intellectual."

Yes, mules seem to have an intelli-gence that horses do not. This is demon-strated by their traits of not overeating grain if given the chance, not panicking in a tangle and pooping in designated areas (which they've tried to teach the horse, who only half-heartedly, or half-hockily, has adopted).

Mules, unlike horses, also play by the rules. Often *their* rules, but they always color within the lines. During Hurricane Floyd of 1999, the coastal plain of North Carolina was hit hard. Torrential rain was followed by mas-sive flooding. Huge sec-tions of the flat plain were underwater. Dale and Jim had their prop-erty inundated. They salvaged what they could from the house and led their four mules out to the road in knee-deep water toward safety. The mules balked at the property line. Dale's "house rules" forbade the mules to cross that imag-inary obstacle. They freed the mules, thinking when the water got high enough, they'd find a way out. But next morning the mules were back in the barn and the water was up to their backs. Jim haltered the boss mule and tied him to the transom of a 16-foot boat with a 25-horsepower Evinrude. They putted out toward the road. The mule came right along until he reached the edge of the property. He dug in all four feet and stopped the parade.

Jim was twistin' the throttle and fish-tailin', but goin' nowhere. Then surely but steadily, Boss mule backed clear to the barn, towing the sputtering ship like he was reeling in a 400-pound catfish.

But mules do like to have fun. Jackson Hole Jerry had a big mule that liked to stand in the back of his little two-horse trailer. Jerry came home one day to find the trailer at the bottom of the slope below the house. "Who moved the trailer?" he asked his wife. "Not me," she said. Jerry hooked up and pulled it back to the top of the field. He unhooked, started for the house and looked back to find his big mule clomping into the trailer. The tongue lifted off the ground and down the hill he went.

Jerry thought he heard him laughing! 🐎

On The Edge Of Common Sense

By Baxter Black, D.V.M.

COW ATTACK

Illustration by Wally Badgett

"*What happened to your pickup seat? Is that buffalo track?*"
  Well, I guess you had to be there. We had a cow attack.
It all began when me and Roy went out to check the cows.
  We'd finished lunch and watched our "soap" and forced ourselves to rouse.

We's pokin' through the heavy bunch for calves to tag and check.
  I spotted one but his ol' mom was bowin' up her neck.
She pawed the ground and swung her head a-slingin' froth and spit
  Then bellered like a wounded bull. "Say, Roy," I says, "Let's quit!"

But Roy was bent on taggin' him and thought to make a grab.
  "Just drive up there beside the calf, I'll pull him in the cab."
Oh, great. Another stroke of genius, of cowboy derring-do.
  Sure-'nuff when Roy nabbed the calf, his mama came in, too.

And I do mean climbed up in there! Got a foot behind the seat
  Punched a horn right through the windshield and she wasn't very neat.
She was blowin' stuff out both ends till the cab was slick and green
  It was on the floor and on the roof and on the calf vaccine.

If you've been inside a dryer at the local laundromat
  With a bear and 50 horseshoes then you know just where I's at.
At one point she was sittin' up, just goin' for a ride
  But then she tore the gun rack down. The calf went out my side.

I was fightin' with my door lock which she'd smashed a-passin' by
  When she peeked up through the steering wheel and looked me in the eye.
We escaped like paratroopers out the window, landed clear.
  But the cow just kept on drivin', 'cause the truck was still in gear.

She topped a hump and disappeared. The blinker light came on
  But if she turned I never saw, by then the truck was gone.
I looked at Roy, "My truck is wrecked. My coveralls are soaked.
  I'll probably never hear again. I think my elbow's broke.

"And look at you—yer pitful. All crumpled up and stiff
  Like you been et by wild dogs and pooped over a cliff."
"But think about it," Roy said. "Since Grampa was alive,
  I b'lieve that that's the firstest time I've seen a cattle drive." 🐎

ON THE EDGE OF COMMON SENSE | BY BAXTER BLACK

Cripple Creek Calvin and the Snakey Mare

ILLUSTRATION BY KEVIN CORDTZ

Calvin said he wasn't that good at gettin' hurt. Of course, some would say he didn't have to try that hard. He's still ridin' broncy horses even though his deductible is up to $45,000.

Some would've thought he should've waited more than 2 months after the knee surgery to try out the snakey mare; at least he started in the round corral. Some would say that naming his North Carolina ranch the Cripple Creek Livestock Company became a self-fulfilling prophecy. It explained his perpetual lameness.

The snakey mare was 8 years old. Calvin knew her well. In anticipation he'd asked the doctor to leave him some medial movement in his knee, so he wouldn't always be jabbin' his horse with a spur. Good thinkin'.

He'd made several circles inside the round pen when his grandson came to watch. "Hi, Pawpaw!"

Calvin stopped the mare in front of the boy. "My bloodline," thought Calvin. "He'll be out here someday, and I'll be leanin' on the fence."

"Make him wun, Pawpaw!"

"Naw, I...," he started to say, as he shifted in the saddle to pat the boy on the back. Sensing Calvin's vulnerability, the mare bogged her head and commenced to bucking! She'd been savin' up and had plenty. Calvin never really got in rhythm with her. The grandson was heard to remark afterward that Pawpaw looked like a Slinky® goin' down the stairs.

It'd been a long time since Calvin had heard a bronc bawl like that. It was an eerie sound: a cross between an elk bugle and a lion's roar, with a twang of tortured mule in there somewhere. She crashed to her knees, pitching Calvin forward over her neck. Then she reared back and rose up. Calvin would've mercifully fallen off except that his belt hooked over the saddle horn! Some would say the next few seconds were reminiscent of a frenzied mating ritual involving a sea otter and a fire hose.

Calvin, in retelling of his final descent, remarked on a Zen-like experience where everything became slow motion. He flashed back on the memory of his friend, Monica, a barrel racer. She, too, had gotten over the top of her horse on the last barrel and hooked the front of her bra over the saddle horn. Calvin remembered thinking that surely those puny hooks would break, not thinking it through that Monica was a full-figured woman and had industrial-strength hardware 6 inches wide across her back. She crossed the finish line lying on the horse like a surfboard.

The memory of Monica faded....

Calvin's meteor-like impact was slowed only when he tangled an arm in the coils of his rope on the way down, which flipped him over, allowing him to land feet first...on his bad knee. He did the splits, injuring a groin muscle.

The grandson clapped.

Some would say it was the end of a perfect cowboy day.

On the Edge of Common Sense

By Baxter Black

Butch and Chope

Illustration by J.P. Rankin

BUTCH HAS a theory about hard-core, born-to-rope ropers: As soon as they build a loop and take one swing, it kicks their brain out of gear.

To demonstrate how this theory works, he told me about a friend of his. We'll call him Chope.

Butch was runnin' a ranch in the wilds of New Mexico east of Las Vegas. He'd bought a set of braymer bulls to put on his braymer cows, and one of the bulls had turned out to be a bad actor. He'd sure-'nuff do some damage if you cornered him.

They had occasion to sort off some of the bulls. They gathered 'em in a corral along with whatever cows came along. As they were workin' the cows out the gate, one of the bulls kept tryin' to escape. It was that sure-'nuff bad bull. Chope was horse-back watchin' the gate. The third time the bull tried to slip out, Chope, who was tied on hard and fast, slapped a loop on him.

The bull turned and thundered back across the corral. Chope pitched the slack and was tryin' to square his horse around when the bull hit the end of the line. All 1,400 pounds of him.

Chope's horse had only got halfway around and was sideways to the bull when the slack ran out. He was slammed to the ground! Butch said he could see that nylon rope stretched an extra 5 feet as the bull was lifted off his front quarters till he looked like Trigger. At that same moment they heard a sound like Mickey Mantle drivin' one over the centerfield fence. The saddle horn had broken off!

The rope with saddle horn attached cracked like a whip and lashed straight for a horse tied to the fence. It just missed a dismounted cowboy and coiled around the horse's pommel and saddle horn. The tail with Chope's horn still attached whopped the horse's butt. The horse bucked loose, breakin' his reins, and the bull galloped off draggin' the line.

Butch looked at Chope madly tyin' another rope to his saddle through the gullet.

"Whattya doin'?" asked Butch.

"I'm gonna rope him and get my rope back," answered Chope.

Butch stared at him. His broken saddle sat cockeyed, his hat was gone. His poor horse was shakin' like a front row spectator at a fireworks extravaganza. You could almost hear his ears ringin'. It was like Chope was lashing the horse to the end of a harpoon line.

Butch placed his hand over Chope's and said, "Let's think about this a minute … nobody's dead yet."

On the Edge of Common Sense

By Baxter Black

Mule Days

THERE'S SOMETHING about mule people.

Debra was a recovering horse person married to a deep South good ol' boy name of Lamar. She was also a closet mule person. A local trader was trolling for buyers. He had a Paint gelding, a couple of sturdy saddle horses and an 8-month-old Jericho Jack all displayed in his pasture between the house and the road.

Debbie drove by, looked at the Paint, glanced at the saddle horses and braked hard for the little burro. Thank goodness she had the trailer hooked on and her strapping son handy. The burrito charmed her, the trader held her up

and they loaded him with the warning that he'd never been touched by humans.

Lamar didn't greet their arrival with unbridled enthusiasm. "No way! No time! No how! Not on yo life! Nevuh!"

She had immediately unloaded Burrito in the round corral knowing he would escape from anything less and had been feeding him there since. (It took a full week to persuade Lamar to try and help her halter the beast.)

Now Lamar was purty cowboy and could rope. He got Burrito circling like a man with one oar. It was like trying to rope an emu with antlers. His first loop cleared the ears and front feet and came tight around the flank. Lamar was off balance when the rope jerked. It peeled two square inches of hide off each palm and pulled him over on his nose.

"Go get my ofver wope," he suggested through his split lip.

Debbie came back with his other good rope. Lamar managed to panty hose the burro a second time and lose that lasso as well. They had recently seen the film *The Horse Whisperer*. It was fresh on her mind as she watched the *donkeeto* gallop around the round corral, the two ropes trailing in his wake like crepe paper flying from Ben Hur's chariot. Lamar crumpled to his knees.

Debra spoke. "Reminds me of Robert Redford starring in that great movie. *The Alabama Ass Whisperer*," she said with a straight face.

"Funny," he replied, "very funny."

Mule humor. Elusive — unexpected — dry as an asbestos candy bar.

I was in Bishop, Calif., at a grand celebration of mule people on Memorial Day. They call it Mule Days. I can recommend it. It's kind of like a cowboy poetry gathering … except more intellectual.

On the Edge of Common Sense

BY BAXTER BLACK, DVM

A Woman's Work is Never Done

HE WAS A GOOD DAKOTA RANCHER with the stubborn Norwegian determination that allowed him to break-even in the unforgiving country north of Mobridge.

He raised four children on the ranch. They were his cowboys, farm hands, truck drivers, fence builders and horse breakers. They also learned to cook, sew, can fruit, butcher and do laundry. They were all girls.

I, Baxter Black, have known many farm and ranch families who have had only daughters, or have girls who are better help than the sons. Most dads handle it well and soon realize a girl can run a hay baler, squeeze chute or spirited horse as well as a boy can. But it's a different relationship. There's always his nervous worry that maybe she won't be able to do it, that his expectations are too high.

In the daughter's case, she actually tries harder, and usually becomes better so she can prove herself qualified in his eyes.

Anyway, the daughters of our good Dakota rancher all grew up and married men with no cow knowledge or cowboy skills. They even made poor chore boys. But all the girls lived close enough to the home place to help Dad during the branding, shipping and fall work.

Last October, fate decreed that three of the four girls were unable to attend the gather. The burden fell on Katrina and her dude husband, Norville, a merchant and Lewis and Clark re-enactor.

"Which horse do you want to ride?" asked Katrina.

"Well, none of 'em, really," said Norville.

"Then see if you can catch Rocket," she said.

Thirty minutes later, after Rocket had stepped on, bit and exhausted Norville, the horse was saddled. They rode out and Dad sent them to the northwest corner.

"You take the creek," Katrina instructed Nor. "I'll ride the ridge."

As they finished their circles and met, Norville admitted he had seen two other cows but they wouldn't stay with the bunch.

"You go back and get those two and I'll push in what we've gathered," she said.

Two long hours passed before Norville straggled in with the delinquent cows. Katrina and her dad waited by the gate and watched Norville's arrival. He looked like he had been eaten by Babe the Blue Ox and then regurgitated. His hat was gone, his nose was bloody, both eyes were the color of prune juice and his right sleeve fluttered in tatters.

"I ran into a tree," was his only explanation as he rode by, eyes front.

Katrina explained to her dad how she'd sent Norville back for the two cows. He shook his head.

"You should know by now," he said, "never send a boy to do a woman's job." 🐎

On the edge of common sense

By Baxter Black

Mistaken identity

Illustration by
Boots Reynolds

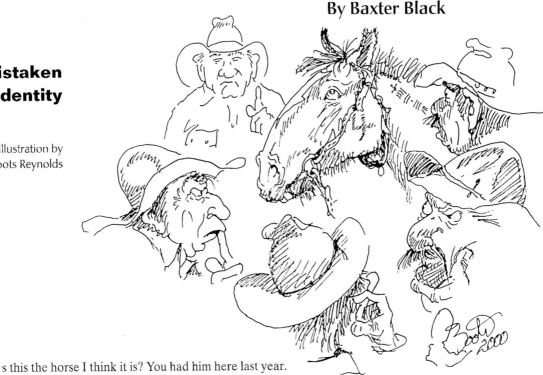

I s this the horse I think it is? You had him here last year.
That rope got tangled in his feet; he jumped just like a deer.
He pulled the brandin' pot plum down and hung up in the gate.
It tore clean off its hinges, which is why it don't hang straight.

    I'm tellin' you I know this horse. He threw you cross the fence!
        The ground crew tried to find a hole and hide in self-defense.
    He bucked back through the cows and calves and tried to kill Joe's truck.
        I've never seen a grille fall off—ol' Joe was thunderstruck.

    He finally stopped to catch his wind, his hide was wringin' wet.
        We tried to slip up next to him, as close as we could get.
    To try and grab a draggin' rein, was all that we could hope,
        But he nearly did a back-flip when Jim Bob shook out a rope.

    I thought that net wire fence would hold, but I sure missed my guess.
        He climbed it like a Sherman tank and lit out toward the west.
    The whole corral was tore up bad, we've fixed it back since then.
        But there's still bite marks on the gate inside the brandin' pen.

    You sure you wuddn't here last year … performed that tour de force?
        "You've got me mixed up with someone. Hell, I just bought this horse."
    By gosh, ol' son, I think yer right—you wuddn't even here.
        It seems like I remember now … Slim rode him here last year.

ON THE EDGE OF COMMON SENSE | BY BAXTER BLACK

Anatomy of a Wreck

It just goes to show you how quickly a walk in the park can turn into a 4-alarm stampede. The only thing that kept the wreck from resulting in permanent damage to man or beast was that the soil on the plains of eastern Colorado is loose and sandy.

Paddy, not his real name, and a couple of neighbors were moving some of his cows from one big pasture to the next. Things were going smoothly, the cows knew the way, the sun was shining, the grass was still holding up good, and what could go wrong?

Paddy was riding his big gray gelding. The kinda horse that can do it all. Even the horse was whistling a tune. Suddenly a dingy heifer broke out of the bunch and turned back. She caught the drovers off guard, squirted between them and headed back where she'd come from. The ball of twine began to unravel.

Paddy whirled the big gray, and in two jumps they were flyin' across the plain. The crew watching could see Paddy and the heifer appear and disappear up and down across the rolling grass prairie. Gray overtook the heifer and they headed back in the direction of the still-plodding herd. The big horse was feeling his oats and had built up a head of steam. The heifer pounded down a sandy ridge, past the watching cowboys, followed by horse and rider. Midway down the side Gray stuck his front feet in the loose dirt and exploded!

He seemed to stand straight up on his front legs; imagine a pole vaulter, a medieval catapult or stepping on a sand rake.

Very few bronc riders could have stayed on, and Paddy was not one of them. There was a scream like someone falling off a cliff, followed by what might've been a giant zipper being opened, a whip cracking, two thuds, a whoop and a crumple.

Old Gray regained his feet, unhurt. Ten feet away Paddy appeared to be standing on his head, shirt down around his shoulder, boots sticking up in the air and completely pantless! He keeled over like a felled tree.

During the cleanup they deduced that when Paddy was ejected he must have hung his belt buckle on the saddle horn, because his jeans were torn completely off

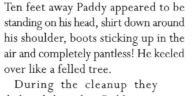

his body. It took two of them to pull his hat back off his nose and a set of wire butter to get the sagebrush out of his ear.

The lady who told me the story was an artist, but she'd never been able to paint the picture. She said she couldn't ever get the flames just right. 🐎

On The Edge Of Common Sense

By Baxter Black, D.V.M.

BRAYMER BAIT

Illustration by Wally Badgett

I STARTED out in the cattle business south of the Little Ear Parallel. That line runs approximately from Fresno to Atlanta. South of that imaginary boundary, cattle with "a little ear" do real well. Braymer and Braymer-cross is what we're talkin' here.

They differ from the European breeds in several ways, particularly in their resistance to hot weather and bugs. But they differ in another important trait that affects the way you handle them. They are not afraid of human beings.

Oh, they'll give us a wide berth given a choice, but they adjust very quickly to the company of men as long as you don't stir 'em up. Which explains why Zebu and not Charolais are worshipped in India. But start messin' with a Santa Gertrudis calf, and you better be lookin' over your shoulder. Or pushin' a sick Braymer . . . he's liable to charge your horse.

As a young and stupid youth, I worked in the feedlots of the Southwest. We fed lots of Braymers. They arrived right out of the swamp or piney woods, or off the desert, and soon adjusted to life at the bunk. But they were not very good patients at the doctor shack. 'Specially after they got to weighin' 600 or 700 pounds.

In spite of my counseling, they got real testy about goin' through the squeeze chute for a little needle and bolus therapy. I can remember actin' as Braymer bait on many occasions.

They'd get on the fight, and one of us would stand in the gate waving like a shipwrecked sailor, trying to entice them out of the pen. Even when sick, they were fast, and I've had more than my share of snot on my shirttail.

My friend Rick said he was attempting to drive a Braymercross cow to the corral. It was hot that spring in the foothills of the Sierra Nevada. He'd pushed the ol' darlin' within a half a mile of the pen when she sulled up and got on the fight. In a moment of brilliance, he roped her. She kept chargin', but he held his dally until they came to a standstill.

He managed to get partner Joe's attention. Joe climbed out of the pickup near the corral, where he'd been waiting, and walked out to Rick. The ol' cow snorted and charged Joe.

Joe lit out for the pickup. "Run to the corral," yelled Rick, spurrin' up behind the cow, holdin' her like a Doberman on a leash.

"Toward the gate!" Joe slowed a couple of times and went down once, but Rick managed to keep her from walkin' Joe like a footlog.

The cow was slobberin' in Joe's pocket when he raced through the gate. Rick undallied as soon as the cow shot in behind Joe. Joe cleared the 5-foot fence from the inside and never hit the top rail!

Which just proves my point—you don't see many Herefords gathered that way, do ya? 🐎

ON THE EDGE OF COMMON SENSE | BY BAXTER BLACK

A Wet Roundup

South of Kansas City, on the Missouri side, it's possible to get into the woods pretty quickly, both geographically and philosophically. It's not easy to gather cows out of that country either.

Randy had called Stevo to help him gather a snorty ol' trader cow off his place. The two of them rode into the quarter-section pasture. "There she is!" said Randy, pointing out a brockle-face angular cow that appeared to have some camel blood in her lineage.

At first site of the two cowboys shakin' out their ropes, the cow headed for the 3-acre tank dam. Randy raced behind her as she started a circum-navigation around the tank to the left. Stevo swung back the other direction to cut her off. On the backside of the tank the riders were charging each other like jousting knights.

Realizing her predicament and using her cow knowledge of a cow-boy's fear of water, the cow veered to starboard and jumped Olympicly into the water. She swam to the middle and stopped. She could still reach bottom, but only her head showed hippo-like on the surface.

"We've got her now!" hollered Randy, rope in hand, dismounting and leaping into an ancient rowboat at water's edge. "Hold my horse!"

Stevo watched incredulously as Randy shoved off and began oaring toward this crocodilian cow. With the ease of a lobsterman roping a buoy, Randy dropped his rope over the cow's head and took half hitches around the bowsprit – thinking, I guess, to tow her in. She had other ideas.

With renewed energy she found her footing on the sea floor and began towing him to the bank. His hat blew off and he fell backward as she gained speed. He resorted to colorful sailor language

till, with oars flailing and spurs jingling, they reached the shore. She actually speeded up once on firm ground.

It's easier for a cow to drag a smooth-bottom rowboat over rough ground than it is to pull a wagon over it, Stevo noted as he watched the odd conveyance careen through rocks, brush, puddles and deadfall that littered the landscape. Stevo actually thought to try to rope the cow, but his good rope horse had never seen a cow pulling a rowboat, and thus refused to participate.

It didn't take long for the boat bottom to disintegrate, leaving Randy riding the keel. Eventually the craft lost its land-worthiness and capsized. The cow escaped, dragging a skeleton of boards and beams, which eventually was her undoing. It allowed her capture 2 hours later when she got hung up in the woods between two saplings and an old still. She'd dried off by then. 🐎

ON THE EDGE OF COMMON SENSE | BY BAXTER BLACK

The 60-Foot Rope

Many moons ago I bought a rawhide reata in Guadalajara. The vaquero that sold it to me demonstrated his throwing technique. He fed out a loop big enough to surround the Boston Celtics, waved a houlihan into it and roped a tamale vendor 30 feet away.

"How long is that rope?" I asked.

"Catorce brazos." El contestó.

Which turned out to be 84' long! I hung it on the wall. I've seen Mexican charros rope in Herraduras using their long lines to thread needles, tiptoe down a horse's back and write their name in the sky. I've been to the Jordan Valley Big Loop where buckaroos carrying more coils than the Wichita lineman tenderly whirled and tossed their twine like fly fisherman front footin' fleet four-legged fillies and fiery fence-jumpin' fresh-broke, full-growed fleabags, frauds, founders, alkali sloggers and snakes in the grass… and made it look pretty.

But 35 feet of medium lay lefthand twist nylon rope always seemed about all I could handle. It worked good in the arena and in the brandin' pen. I actually thought that if I carried more than that I might tangle in the line and be drug to death like Captain Ahab in *Moby Dick*.

I have a few cows. Not enough to make Rob Brown or the Mormon Church jealous, but a few. We gathered last fall but had two big calves and a high-horned red cow break back, go through the fence in a big trap, and head for two sections of rough country. Franciso, Jack and I lit after 'em on a dead run. Ducking the mesquite and cat claw, leapin' and skirtin' the barrel cactus, cholla, and pear, jumpin' the little arroyos and snow plowin' the big ones.

Jack snagged the 450-pound red heifer on a quick turn back and flattened her. I rode up to him to offer assistance. On the next ridge I saw Francisco in full pursuit silhouetted against the sky, runnin' hard, swingin'

his rope, the 525-pound black steer, tail in the air, a horse's length in the lead. Francisco's hat blew off. He threw his loop, and missed. The steer swerved to starboard and headed straight for Jack and me. He burst up out of the arroyo and ran right at my horse! He passed within 6 feet of me in the fast lane goin' the opposite direction at the speed of a cheetah. I threw my rope, bingo! The coils peeled out of my hand like he'd fallen off a cliff!

It occurred to me 10 minutes later, as I was crawling around on my hands and knees in the mesquite thicket trying to catch the dragging end of my rope, that had I been tied-on or actually caught my dallies, I'd probably been pulled over backward and smashed flat.

But the longer I had to crawl after that rope, the more I began to appreciate the value of an extra 20 feet.

It takes a long time to learn to be a cowboy. 🐴

On the Edge of Common Sense

By Baxter Black

Persistence

Illustration by
Don Gill

PERSISTENCE IS a two-sided coin. Charlie asked in town if anyone was needing a cowhand. The horseshoer in the cafe directed him out to Don's ranch. Charlie found Don down at the hay barn and introduced himself, "I hear you might be lookin' for help."

"By gosh, son, ya showed up right on time, my shoulder's sore and givin' me trouble. I could sure use help feedin', calvin' heifers and ridin' the heavy bunch. You can ride Rancid, over there."

Charlie looked at a deep bay gelding with a gray muzzle lolling in a nearby pen. There was something about him that made Charlie ask, "Does he buck?"

Don winced imperceptibly, "Oh, he's got a playful streak. I broke him as a 2-year-old. He was big then. Bucked me off more than once before I got him sold to a high-school teacher in Rupert.

He kept him for six days and then brought him back. Suggested I take him to the buckin'-horse sale in Miles City.

"I chuckled at that. I figgered if I stayed at it and worked him easy he'd quit that buckin'. He's such a good horse to cover the country on. Big and stout and strong. He did try me, though. Rattled my teeth and hung me over a rail fence like wet laundry. He unseated me six times that first week I got him back. Then he threw me into a beaver dam.

"So I just gave him to an outfitter in Mackay. He kept him for five years. Rode him twice, I think. But he lost his business and since he never paid me, he brought him back. First day I took him on a long circle clear up there by that stand of quakies." Don pointed to the foothills behind him. "He was a real gentleman. I relaxed thinkin' maybe he'd mellowed. Caught me off guard. Pitched me into the fork of a tree.

"I took after him with a vengeance. I wore him out. He did pretty good after that but I had to watch him all the time. He'd still try and throw me off and sometimes he did, but I figgered sooner or later he'd gentle down or give up."

"How old is he?" asked Charlie.

Don kinda drew a little circle in the dirt with the toe of his boot and looked over at the horse who seemed to be enjoying the conversation. "Sixteen," he said.

There was a pregnant silence, then Charlie asked, "Your shoulder?"

"Yup," nodded Don.

Charlie studied Don a minute. "Who named him Rancid?"

A pause.

"Everyone." 🐎

ON THE EDGE OF COMMON SENSE | BY BAXTER BLACK

Go Catch My Horse

In the old days I resigned myself that bad luck came in threes, i.e., three flat tires, three smashed fingers or three social faux pas. It's comforting to know that good ol' Dakota Mike is still proving my theory. And, I'm not even counting the initial injury that resulted in a swollen right knee, which put him down for a solid week.

It was very bad timing, since he was calving heifers and was very particular about tagging and vaccinating newborns and kept meticulous records. His darling wife fed before and after her town job, but couldn't do the horseback heifer check. But she did notice the hole in the wire fence had allowed some mixing. Dakota Mike paced in place and fretted until Saturday when she could help him catch up.

With her help, he saddled Forrest, a bay mustang-plow-horse cross they named after Forrest Gump. He was big and gentle, but not a quick learner. She rode Pony. Mike loaded his saddlebag with tags, vaccine and syringes. He figured he could pack the nearly empty spindle of barbed wire. Darlin' would carry the fence-stretcher and pliers. He stood on the tie pile to mount. Wincing, he got his right leg swung over the saddle and gently maneuvered his tennis-shoed foot into the right stirrup. He squared up and eased Forrest beside the pickup where he'd preplaced the wire roll.

He reached down with his right hand and picked up the wire. The loose roll made a queer rattling sound — one that Forrest recognized from the rattlesnake program on the Discovery Channel. He hunched and fired straight back with both hind legs! Mike had his left hand outstretched with the reins, his right hand outstretched with the wire, his left foot in the stirrup, and his noodle right leg hanging limp. In the time it took him to realize he should drop the wire and grab the horn, Forrest had punched him into a two-point landing under Pony's feet. Darlin' leaned over and asked, "Are you alright?"

"Go catch my horse," he said, palpating his scraped forehead and sore right shoulder.

With the fence repaired, they rode into the heifers. Mike prided himself on his cows' mothering instinct. He creaked off his horse, noting the nearby mamma cow pawing the ground, and quietly snuck up, with loaded ear-tagger and syringe, on a still-wet newborn. He carefully dropped down on the calf with one knee. In a blinding flash he was flying backward, banging his head on the frozen cowpies and filling his collar with muck.

"Are you alright?" Darlin' asked.

"Go catch my horse," he said.

Across the pasture he again detached himself from Forrest and approached another newborn. Not seeing the mother, he managed to straddle this one and was supporting it between his trembling limbs. He felt something in his crotch and looked down. A black nose and muzzle the exact size and width of a cow's head protruded between his legs. In less time than he could put two and two together, he was catapulted in a flailing arc 10 feet in front of the calf and had somehow managed to ear-tag his left pant leg.

"Are you alright?" Darlin' asked.

"Go...," he grunted.

"I know," she said, "I know." 🐎

ON THE EDGE OF COMMON SENSE | BY BAXTER BLACK

The Old Gray Mare

Ray was known to be a good Thoroughbred trainer. Because of his reputation, he was given a 2-year-old gray filly whose brother had raced well and made money. However, the owner claimed that his boys couldn't break her to ride.

Ray was up to the challenge. He saddled her with his heels. She broke in two, he made three jumps and she planted him in the dirt! Three times a day for 2 weeks she bucked him off. Ray invited every cowboy within 20 miles of Tarpon Springs to try her. No score.

One day the veterinarian was out to his place, so Ray had him tranquilize the gray filly. He saddled her. "I'll get ya this time," he said as she leaned stuporously against the stall wall. He stumbled her into the round pen and climbed on. He cut her into the counterclockwise direction and made a full circle. He relaxed just a fraction, then turned her back the other way. She stuck her nose between her front feet and ejected Ray like he'd been fired from God's own slingshot!

Ray was bemoaning his problem to Johnny Boy, a local cowboy. "Well, I'll bet we can snub her to Brownie and break her." Brownie was a linebacker of a horse, 15 1/2 hands tall, No. 2 shoes, out of the Peterbilt/Kenworth line, which suited Johnny just fine 'cause he himself was big as a young mule.

Johnny Boy showed up on Brownie the next day ridin' his brand-new, still-squeakin', pigeon-toed Bona Allen saddle. The riggin', latigo and cinches were showroom stiff, but as tight as Johnny could get 'em. Gray was saddled and the halter left on under the hackamore. Johnny Boy tied the halter rope to his brand-new saddle horn with 2 feet of lead. Ray climbed aboard Gray. Johnny Boy dropped Brownie in compound, and let out the clutch. The filly set her feet and skidded like a four-legged skier up the bunny hill towrope.

There are moments of great expectation in life. Waiting for the curtain to open on a great stage play, hearing a shotgun shell being levered into the chamber, watching a short fuse burn on a box of dynamite.

The filly exploded! She sprang at Brownie! Left front across the swells, right front across the cantle! Ray dove one way, Johnny the other! She stripped the saddle off over Brownie's head and drug it around the pen, managing to stomp and slash her signature into the new leather.

Johnny Boy stood dumbfounded. Brownie had noogies, his brand new Bona Allen looked like something a tyrannosaurus threw up, and his shirt was torn down the back in two pieces, each with a sleeve.

Ray didn't get to hear all of Johnny's complaints because he'd still be digging sand out of his ears for the next 2 days. 🐎

BAXTER BLACK

ON THE EDGE OF COMMON SENSE

SHOEIN' PIGEYE

Illustration by Boots Reynolds

"Just count me out," said Wilford as he lay there in the dirt,
  A shoein' rasp behind his ear, a hoof print on his shirt.
"I'll handle this," said Freddie, "You jus' git outta the way.
  This sorry bag of buzzard bait has met his match today."

The horse weren't much to look at, just the kind a trader'd buy
  But you knew that he'd be trouble when you looked him in the eye.
It was small and mean and glittered, as deep as Jacob's well,
  Like lookin' down the smoke stack of the furnace room in Hell.

Freddie grabbed a set of nippers and bent to grab a hoof.
  When he woke up . . . his shoein' chaps were danglin' from the roof.
His shirt tail hung in tatters and his watch had come unwound.
  The nippers' orbit finally peaked. They clattered to the ground.

"You get a twitch," said Freddie, "I'm about to clean his clock."
  He tied a rope around a rock and fished it past the hock
Then pulled back on the sideline to instill a little fear
  When Pigeye bit a good sized chunk from Wilford's offside ear.

Wilford tangled in the sideline and tried to navigate
  While draggin' 'round the horse corral like alligator bait.
Freddie tried to stop this trollin' with a loop around the head,
  And it mighta worked if Freddie'd only roped the horse instead.

But of course he caught pore Wilford, who left a funny track . . .
  . . . Sorta like an oil slick, when Freddie jerked the slack.
By now the boys were testy and tired of this travail
  They figgered they'd be done by noon but they'd not drove a nail.

"Go git the boss's Humvee! We'll winch him to a post."
  They got the cayuse necked up tight, and set to work . . . almost
'Cause the halter broke and Pigeye walked the length of Freddie's back.
  They rolled beneath the axle like two lovers in the sack.

Freddie heard the sound of gunfire like a thousand rifle choirs,
  "I've got the sucker pinned down, Fred, I shot out all the tires!"
It was dark when Wilford stood up and laid his hammer down
  A gross of crooked horseshoe nails lay scattered all around.

The place looked like a cross between the tomb of Gen'ral Grant
  And a Puppy Chow explosion at the Alpo dog food plant!
Wilford couldn't move his elbow but he grinned and proudly said,
  "Ol' Pard, we done a good day's work," to what was left of Fred.

"Just look at that there shoein' job. Them clinches in a row.
  It's such a good example we could make a video."
Freddie crawled out from the wreckage and staggered to one knee,
  "What say we wait till mornin' to put on the other three. . . . ?"

ON THE EDGE OF COMMON SENSE | BY BAXTER BLACK

Kelley and the Super Cowboy

"You could use a little help," the boss told Kelley one morning at the horse barn. "I know yer doin' a good job, but sometimes an extra hand can make it easier. Besides, the kid needs the work; although I'm told he's a super cowboy, he's in a slump."

The "kid" turned out to be a down-on-his-luck bronc rider on whom the boss had taken pity. His bad luck hadn't affected his super-cowboy confidence, though. "I kin ride anything with hair and, if I may say, I'm a good hand with a rope…if you've got an extry I could borrow," said the kid upon meeting Kelley the first time.

That next day Kelley rigged up the kid with one of the boss's saddles, a headstall and an extra rope. The only gear the kid had with him was a hack rein, rodeo chaps and a bronc saddle, none of which had much value for ranch work.

They rode into the foggy coastal California morning to gather a bull and a cow-calf pair. At first sight of the cowboys, the bull ran for cover. They tried

to turn him back to no avail. "Rope him," said Kelley. The super cowboy missed. Kelley managed to catch a head and a front leg. The kid missed a couple more till Kelley finally told him to get behind and push.

Half an hour later they came back for the pair, a big, high-horned, rangy-lookin' yellow cow that easily weighed 1,400 pounds, and her 2-month-old calf. With surprising ease they got them all the way across the verdant hillside pasture to the gate. Then suddenly the cow whirled, dived between them and headed back to the oak trees. Kelley swung a quick loop and snagged the calf. He was off his horse and on the calf quicker than a tarantula wasp, and tied him down. He looked around to ask the kid's help dragging the bawling calf through the gate. Then all they'd have to do was wait for mama cow to come back and claim her baby.

But the kid had taken it upon himself to catch the cow. Kelley watched as he raced across the damp pasture accompanied by his two Border Collies in pursuit

of the high-tailin' cow. Kelley noticed the kid was a fearless rider. The cow slipped on the wet ground and went down momentarily. The kid rode by at a high lope, dropped his loop over the cow's head and tried to swing his horse around. Not in time. The cow rose, the dally missed, the horse stumbled. It was a great wreck. A twinge of admiration crossed Kelley's mind as he saw the kid jerked from the saddle, both hands on the rope, and go sailing after the cow.

Kelley watched unbelieving as the cow thundered across the slick grass draggin' the super cowboy like a tuna tied behind a speedboat. They were headed right for the calf. Completing the scene came the two super cow dogs in the rear, drivin' the horse, fenders flappin', tail ringin' and reins flyin' in the wake of the cow and her tenacious passenger.

"How's the kid workin' out?" the boss asked Kelley later.

"Fine. Just fine," answered Kelley, with the smile of a man who'd found another source of great cowboy memories for future exaggeration and retelling.

On the Edge of Common Sense

By Baxter Black

Immortal Branding

Illustration by
Kevin Cordtz

I GOT BUCKED off the other day, alas it was nothing new.
I's settin' on a borrowed horse, the rope was old, the bruise is blue.

Thank goodness everyone was there, they never miss a branding.
The geezers come just to help out but nothing too demanding.

They mostly come to catch firsthand some wreck or temper riling.
I guess I really made their day, I saw they all were smiling.

I'd double-hocked a heifer calf and started for the flankers
But they were backed up, left no time to toss out my anchors.

My dally slipped, she took the slack, and started to skidaddle.
The rope flipped up across my waist and slicked me off the saddle.

Just like I'd rode beneath a tree or hit a power line.
I lit and rolled and bounced back up like everything was fine.

The geezers gathered round and asked "Hurt?" "Nope," I lied, "it doesn't."
They seemed so disappointed. Was like they were hurt I wasn't.

But they'd make do. Ya see, the seed of the story was planted.
For weeks my rep would be discussed with n'er a mercy granted.

Yes, history was set on course, no doubt to be rewritten
Each time a geezer told the tale. In truth it's only fittin'

'Cause that's how Pecos Bill was born and Wyatt Earp and others
Like Pancho Villa, Sitting Bull, Will Pickett and his brothers.

Charles Goodnight, Casey Tibbs, we bid *vaya con Dios,*
All legends in our cowboy world we honor now as heroes.

So my mishap could be the start of my own legacy
That years from now will see great marble statues carved of me.

My picture framed will hang on walls, my likeness carved in leather,
My name will be a household word wherever cowboys gather.

But in the meantime I must bear the taunts and jibes that linger
Of when I bucked off some kid's horse and broke my little finger.

On the Edge of Common Sense

By Baxter Black

The Haflinger deal

Illustration by Don Gill

TWO JUMPS has a long history of famous horse trades in his native Tennessee. According to him, at one time or another he could have owned Doc Bar, Gallant Fox, Midnight Sun, Naborr, Fury, Trigger, Pegasus, and a big gelding offered to him by an enlisted man in the Trojan Army. But things just didn't work out.

More typical was his Appaloosa-Haflinger trade. A feller from up the holler named Mr. Salchucker owned a team of Haflingers. For those of y'all who are unusual-equine impaired, they are a breed of draft ponies. Good, stout horses, maybe 14 hands and useful for pullin' things in tight places.

According to Two Jumps, Mr. Salchucker had used them to pull a wagon, but he was willin' to trade these splendid log pullers for an Appy mare that had been on display in Two Jumps' front pasture by the road.

Two Jumps had seen the Haflingers and thought they looked pretty flashy, so a deal was made.

On delivery, Two Jumps hooked them up to his nice little surrey for a test drive. Then the phone rang in the barn. Two Jumps answered, and it was one of the local irritants. This is the kind of feller that will call and talk for hours about your horses or cows or land or Haflingers but never buy anything.

Durin' the conversation, Leroy, Two Jumps' resident horse trading consultant and test crash dummy, wandered in and pointed at the Haflingers tied outside. Meaning, could he take them for a spin?

Two Jumps covered the mouthpiece and said, "Sure, but take them to the arena. I'm not sure how broke they are."

Fifteen minutes later while Two Jumps was still scratching the local irritant, Leroy stumbled back through the barn door. His shirt was ripped off, his hat looked like a hippopotamus cud, and one spur was bent sideways.

Leroy's story, as embellished by Two Jumps, was as follows:

"They seemed calm enough so I took 'em out through the pasture. Pusher (the miniature stud horse) came over the hill ... spooked 'em all ... broke for the woods ... and Two Jumps, part of your surrey is in the pond ... part of your surrey is in the cedar tree ... and I don't know where the other part is!"

Two Jumps got a call 10 days later from an officious-sounding gentleman in Franklin. He had heard of the Haflingers and was interested in buying, but "... wouldn't pay more than a thousand apiece."

Perfect timing, thought Two Jumps, who had just unloaded them at the Murfreesboro sale barn last weekend. For $250.

ON THE EDGE OF COMMON SENSE | BY BAXTER BLACK

Mule Conversion

What makes a man switch from horses to mules? Loneliness? Desperation? Boredom? Something to fulfill his life after he quits chewing Copenhagen?

Deb has watched Jimmy make the change. She actually may have contributed to his fall, which makes her an accessory, because she bought him a carriage for Christmas. She hadn't known he'd been fantasizing about jacks and jennies the same way teamsters fantasize about Reos and Kenworths.

Jimmy started going to buggy and wagon sales, draft-horse shows, Amish rodeos. He started learning the names of things, doubletrees, neck yokes, spacers, tugs, sulkies, lines, gees, haws, hitches, hames, contusions, fractures, sprains, bolsters, blinders, britches, and bruises. He began experimenting. Maybe it was the challenge that appealed to him…dealing with an equal.

Deb had gone to Amarillo shopping. Upon returning, her 15-year old son, Will, met her at the door. She could tell something was wrong. "Dad's had a small wreck," he said. "He tried four-up, didn't he?" she asked. Will nodded. "Which ones did he use?"

It turned out Jimmy had hitched George and Huey, 2-year-old mules weighing about 700 pounds each, with Dolly and Patsy, full-grown, well-broke mules at 1,500 pounds each, to a big rubber-tired flatbed hay wagon. Jimmy wasn't exactly sure which pair should be in front, so he put the big broke mules in the lead. As Custer would say, "I didn't know."

Jimmy didn't have a complete set of harnesses for four-up, so he improvised with doubled-over baling wire, hay twine, old saddle parts, an inner tube, hog rings, an elevator belt, u-bolts, waterskiing tow rope, and the frayed electrical cord off a broken belt sander. He showed son Will how to work the brake and admonished him to never jump off.

With Jimmy ahold of the lines and young Will with a death grip on the brake, they eased out into the pasture. The jury-rigged chains on the wheel horse doubletree began slappin' and bangin'. It spooked the young mules. Jimmy, who had never driven four-up was still tryin' to get the eight lines sorted out. He looked like a man rassling an octopus. Dolly and Patsy took advantage and were soon pounding across the soft ground like thundering buffalo! George and Huey were trying to keep up. Will was mashing on the brake with all his might and Jimmy was shouting, "DON'T JUMP OFF! DON'T JUMP OFF!" They ran until the young mules simply quit, and started dragging their feet. They plowed to a stop with George and Huey sort of wadded up against the wagon.

Thanks to Ace Reid, the patron saint of cowboys, neither mule nor man was hurt except for the blisters between Jimmy's fingers and Will's dog, who sprained an ankle jumping from the wagon at full speed.

Deb says that Jimmy's next major project will be a 20-mule team hitch. Right now he's savin' up hog rings and baling wire. Should be good. I just hope the dog heals up in time. 🐎

On the Edge
of Common Sense

By Baxter Black

The Proud Cut Holstein Steer

Illustration by Boots Reynolds

I'LL NEVER know just how I got that proud cut Holstein steer.
  I'd rather have lasagna fingers wiggled in my ear
Or get caught eating tofu at the Cattlemen's Hotel
  Than spend another minute with that Holstein steer from hell.

I put him out to grass with some I'd taken on the gain.
  He soon became the Holstein image of Saddam Hussein.
Most cattlemen I know would never make the same mistake
  'Cause steers like him are meaner than a constipated snake.

One afternoon I drove out to inspect this herd of mine.
  The dog jumped out and vanished, but like stink bait on the line
He soon bobbed to the surface like he'd hooked Free Willy's tail,
  Behind him, jaws a 'snappin', came the Holstein killer whale!

I ducked behind a sagebrush but the dog jumped in the cab.
  What followed was a battle like this truck had never had.
Imagine if a coal train pullin' 60 cars in back,
  Doin' 90 miles an hour hit a beer can on the track.

I heard the metal crumple, heard the plastic rip and tear,
  I heard the tires exploding, felt things flyin' through the air.
The dog just kept on barkin' so the steer stayed on the fight,
  Then Lancelot came chargin' up to save me from my plight.

This knight in shining armor was, in fact, to put it blunt,
  My wife in her new tractor with a bale spear on the front.
Distracted by the tractor, the steer came to a stop.
  I raced back to the pickup and clambered up on top.

"Up here!" I hollered loudly, "You can lift me with the spear!"
  The steer came back like bad news, but my wife had heard me clear.
But her aim . . . (I hollered, "Higher!") was a foot or two off tilt,
  She punched right through the truck door and she rammed it to the hilt!

She pulled back on the lever and we all rose overhead.
  I say "we all" because the steer had jumped up in the bed.
The last thing I remember just before I pulled the pin
  was Holstein halitosis and the roof a-cavin' in.

I'm still not sure what happened. I was knocked out cold as toast.
  I woke up feelin' dizzy, propped against a cedar post.
The dog was lookin' nauseous there behind the steering wheel,
  The pickup . . . think Titanic, was a mass of twisted steel.

And what about that proud cut, man eatin', truck stompin', dog kickin',
  Never backin' up polled heavyweight
Holstein steer from hell?
  Well, only time will tell.

But with huntin' season comin' up his fate is cut and dried.
  He's goin' out to pasture with a bull's-eye on his side.

> **On the Edge of Common Sense**   BY **BAXTER BLACK, DVM**

The Eight-Count

"ISN'T THAT LARRY'S HEIFER?" ASKED DICK.

The 2-year-old black whiteface was running down the fenceline along Highway 90. Traffic was moderate on the four-lane highway. The shoulder was not smooth. Arroyos and ridges thick with rocks and brush made any chase risky.

"Pull over!" said Dick to his wife.

The south gate was new. It had a cattle guard, but no cattle gate beside it. Dick jumped out and turned the frightened cow back to the north.

"Call Larry!" he shouted to his wife.

Larry's wife took the call. Within five minutes, Larry had appeared and stationed himself by the north gate to turn the heifer. She was smart enough, or scared enough, to stay off the highway, but she became unreasonable. Larry knew her well. She would actually eat feed out of his hand. He was surprised by her rowdy behavior.

It is a common flaw in cowmen. They form opinions about specific animals. They come to trust them. I've seen grown men (like me) put 2-year-old kids on the back of tame Brahma bulls. But cows can revert to their primitive behavior origins. I don't mean baby calf. I mean buffalo, mastodon, Tyrannosaurus holstein! It is a scientific phenomenon called "getting on the fight."

Some external stimulus or internal metabolic reaction can change a gentle herbivore into a maddened beast. We see this in other species: rabid dogs, a locoed horse or a 4-H parent whose child's pig didn't win grand champion.

Anyway, Larry stood his ground, a few feet beyond the gate. The heifer was running full speed. He spoke to her, actually held out his hand as she approached him at the speed of beef! In his mind, despite the

obvious, he must have thought she would remember their relationship and settle down.

Dick said she hit Larry full frontal right in the chest. He went backwards like she'd pushed him off a cliff. Then, she stood above him, between his legs, looking down at his face. Maybe she recognized him . . . who knows?

About that time, Dick spooked her and she ran right through the fence. Larry lay there flat.

"Can you get up?" asked Dick.

"I tried to," said Larry, "but the ref was just counting four. I decided to wait for the eight-count." 🐴

KEVIN CORDTZ

On the Edge of Common Sense

By Baxter Black

Disappearing Digits

DAR LA VUELTA—*to give a turn. The Mexican roping term passed on to gringos, who bastardized it to "dally." After roping a bovine, the tail of the rope still in your hand is wrapped once around the saddle horn and held. Some think it is safer than being tied hard and fast to the saddle horn. But dallying has its dangers. Should you accidentally get a thumb or finger between the rope and the horn . . . well . . . that's what this commentary is about.*

When Winston Churchill and Richard Nixon made the victory sign, you probably thought the same thing I did—them boys ain't team ropers!

Come to think of it, I've never seen a roper point at the TV camera and say, "We're number one."

Ropers are at a definite disadvantage hitchhiking, buttoning a shirt, and eating with chopsticks.

Many a roper has fished a finger out of his glove as a result of a slipshod dally. It always gives me a queasy feeling to see some roper on his hands and knees searching through the arena dirt like he was lookin' for a contact lens.

In any group of ropers you're liable to find a sampling of fellers who can't count to 10. Most take it in good stride and don't dwell on the handicap of missing a digit or two. It's the price you pay. As they say, "If you ain't been bucked off, cowboy, then you ain't been on many!"

I've still got all my fingers and thumbs, so bein' a sorry roper has its advantages. You gotta catch 'em to lose 'em!

Losing a finger or thumb in the dally is no laughing matter. It's a lot more permanent than getting a haircut. Modern medicine and skilled surgeons can often replace the severed phalange. Of course, the success of the operation depends on the condition of the missing piece and whether you can find it.

Young John walked into the emergency room with his hand wrapped in a towel.

"What happened?" the doctor asked.

"We were brandin' at the Pocket. I roped a calf and hung my thumb in the dally."

"Well, let me see the piece you cut off," said the doc.

"I didn't bring it."

"Do you know where it is? If it's in good shape we might be able to save it."

"Yeah, I do. But when it popped off, it sailed out over my horse's head pretty as you please. My good dog jumped up and snagged it in midair."

"Great Scott, son! Whyn't you shoot the dog?"

"Shoot the dog? He's the best one we got!"

Illustration by Don Gill

ON THE EDGE OF COMMON SENSE | BY BAXTER BLACK

Hat Burning

"How did you set yer hat on fire? Suck starting a Harley?"
"Well, I didn't do it on purpose." His eyebrows were scorched
and gnarly.
His mustache was singed off, uneven and unsymmetrically skewed
While the glass was gone from his glasses, which rendered him
spectacly nude.
"Dark," he said, "You know methane will burn? Me and
Jake were out checkin' the stock.
We were comin' in late and found one that looked like
she needed the doc.
But we were both cow paramedics trained to more than
just ride
And savvied her dire situation all bloated and laid on
her side.
Not having a trocar or bloat hose, first choices for saving
her life,
I blindly palpated the left flank for the place where I'd
plunge my knife.
I inserted the point of my sticker, it fit like
a key in a latch
When Jake said, 'Here let me help you!'
With a flourish the fool struck a match.
A blue flame roared out of the orfice like
St. Helens come back from the dead!
The whoosh, like an airbag exploding
pinned my ears back on my head!
What kept us from burning too
badly, or at least to me it
makes sense,
Was the fireball of
flammable gasses
was mixed with the
rumen contents.
Poor Jake took the blast
a full frontal though
his moustache pro-
tected his lips,
When he took his hat
off of his bald head,
he looked like
a partial eclipse.
The fireball waned
down to a flicker.
The cow was
now lookin' plum flat.

My chest was all greenish and sticky…I could see by the light
of my hat.
But the ultimate insult I suffered wasn't the burnt hat or
the blood,
But my mouth had been opened in protest, and I found I
was chewing her cud!"

On the Edge of Common Sense

By Baxter Black

The Renegade Cow

Just bring 'er on home, the foreman had said,
  That is, if I found her, of course,
In seventeen sections of canyons and brush
  On the back of a nearly broke horse.

Why he even bothered, I'll never know.
  She slipped through the gather each year.
I think he was hopin' that I'd up and quit.
  To a smart man it would have been clear.

Illustration by
Boots Reynolds

But I saddled up and made for the bluffs—
  Think like a cow's how I think.
The creeks had quit runnin', most tanks had gone dry
  So I figgered she'd hunt up a drink.

It was hot as a dashboard in Phoenix in June
  When the Yellow Man Spring come in view.
I was stripped to the skivvies and knee deep in cool,
  When the cow come a-amblin' through.

Whether she jumped the highest or if it was me
  Don't matter 'cause she broke and run.
I swung to the seat slingin' seaweed and moss,
  Thus exposin' my hide to the sun.

She's pickin' a path while I'm building a loop.
  I miss the first five that I throw.
But out on the flat on try number six
  I catch as she's startin' to slow.

I lay on a trap, and she plops to the ground.
  I sideline her right front and rear.
I figger a soakin' will break her to drive.
  My catch rope slips off past her ear.

When all of a sudden my piggin' string's loose!
  She comes off the ground like a rocket.
For a second or two I'm a-straddle her head,
  Then she's blowin' snot in my pocket!

She might've been tired but she plowed quite a while
  Usin' me to turn up the curl.
When she finally got tired of smashin' me flat,
  She left me head-first in the furrow.

That night at the rancho I told the foreman
  I'd bucked off—the story was cleaner.
"That renegade cow?" he asked kinda snooty,
  I just told him that I'd never seen her.

On the Edge of Common Sense

By Baxter Black

Why Cowboy Poetry's Funny

COWBOY POETRY'S mostly funny but, it's just to keep from cryin',
  'Cause the cowboy's life's a constant round of wrecks.
Every time a puncher turns around life blacks him in the eye,
  Or bucks him off or bounces all his checks.

Humiliation's not enough—They get hurt, I mean a lot!
  They've perfected what it takes to set the scene
To create a situation where disaster's guaranteed,
  No matter how the angels intervene.

Think about it. If you really wanted to try and hurt yourself,
  You might call the IRS up for a chat.
Or learn to juggle rattlesnakes, maybe catch 'em with yer teeth,
  Or tell your wife you liked her better fat.

But the cowboy way's a sure bet. First you take a good sized beast,
  A thousand pounds and fit her with some horns
And then make her disposition like a bobcat with the piles
  And give her brains the size of grandpa's corns.

You say, Great! That sure would do it! Put that cowboy with a cow,
  Yer bound to get a wreck you won't forget.
But let's take it a step further and include another brute
  That spooks at shadows and is bigger yet.

One who jumps like Michael Jordan and dives like Moby Dick,
  Then set our cowboy up there on his back.
One more thing, we'll just connect 'em with a piece of nylon rope,
  Then set back and watch our victims come untracked.

Illustration by Boots Reynolds

So that's why us cowboy poets write our humorous refrains,
  'Cause like I said, it's either laugh or cry.
For example, say yer horseback in the brandin' pen one day,
  And see a friend go flyin' through the sky.

We all quick go ridin' over where he's bucked off in the dirt,
  To check his pulse, if there's still one to raise.
And . . . if he's livin' you start tellin' the story right away,
  And if he's dead, you wait a couple days.

ON THE EDGE OF COMMON SENSE | BY BAXTER BLACK

The Broken-Wristed Cowboy

"Carpal tunnel?" I asked the handsome, strapping Utah cowboy, who had both wrists in casts.

"Rodeo," he said. "I bucked off."

"Broncs? Bulls?"

"No, I rode my saddle bronc."

"Did ya win?" I asked.

"Placed third," he said. "They paid two places."

"Oww!" I said, "What happened to your arms?"

"Team roping," he said with a trace of humiliation.

He related that he was a header, but he looked like a heeler to me. Shawn's story unfolded; he was ridin' a horse he'd been trying to break for six years. He'd been buck-free for three weeks. Out they shot from the roper's box like three torpedoes and raced across the arena skimming the high spots.

Shawn reached out and roped the fast-running steer, turned hard to the left and looked back to see if his heeler was close behind. He was ... and saw the whole show. Shawn's horse exploded! To quote him exactly, not "broke in two," "bogged his head" or "blew up" ... "EXPLODED!" He was caught off-guard, leanin' crooked in the saddle and lookin' back. But he stayed dallied up, based on the cowboy theory that "they can't buck if they're dragging somethin'." Wrong.

He blew a stirrup, noted the arena fence closing in, and his rope tied to the steer comin' around the off-side. When Shawn pitched his slack, the horse felt free to really buck. Shawn said he bucked so hard he saw God. Brigham Young was sitting beside Him! It renewed his faith. Brigham spoke to him and said, "Kid, this is going to hurt."

Shawn was leaned out over the northeast quadrant (as you face the temple) when the horse came down front feet first. Our cowboy was fired into the ground like a javelin. The horse thundered on by.

Cowboys rushed to Shawn's aid as he lay there like a drug-runner's Cessna nose-dived into a plowed field in south Florida. Shawn finally managed to stand and recover his "Marlboro Man" mystique.

"You hurt?" they asked.

"No, I'm fine," he said.

"Look at your arms!" the crowd gasped.

Shawn said they curved up midforearm like a camel's foot.

"Man," I said, "what a wreck. Everything that could go wrong did!"

Shawn nodded his head and started to walk away, then turned and said, "Did I tell ya he stepped right square in the middle of my new hat?"

He hadn't, but it did explain the symmetrical Teton Mountain Block and the corrugated edge of the brim. 🐎

On The Edge Of Common Sense

By Baxter Black, D.V.M.

NITWIT WISDOM

Nitwits are partial to wisdom
  that's usually corny and trite.
But the worst part of nitwit wisdom
  is when the nitwit is right!

I's ridin' pastures for Brimhall,
  checkin' for bad eyes and such.
He'd hired this nitwit to help me.
  He never did like me much.

"You can't be good at everything,"
  said Nitwit, missin' the steer.
I had to agree that he wasn't
  good, that is, that much was clear.

I chased the steer and caught his horns,
  I dallied and then I spoke:
"You rope the hocks and we'll stretch him out!"
  He tried, but it was a joke.

"Here, set my horse and hold the head."
  We swapped and I roped the hind.
"Now take back yer horse and hold the heels,
  don't let no slack in yer twine!"

I got off to doctor the steer
  and fished for my last syringe.
When a hoof lashed out and cracked my hand,
  doubled my arm like a hinge!

I stabbed myself with the needle;
  he kicked me under the chin!
Then he rolled me off over backwards,
  drivin' the needle on in.

"Don't let go yer dally! Damn!"
  His rope was floppin' around.
The steer stepped outta the heel loop
  and headed for higher ground.

"You sorry excuse for nothin!
  You line-bred drizzlin' dope!
I guess you saw he's still draggin'
  my brand new 40-foot rope.

"Yer dumber'n boiled gravel.
  I told ya, keep yer slack tight.
Now he'll prob'ly die of pneumonia."
  We watched him flee outta sight.

"Well, look on the bright side," said Nitwit,
  his wisdom cut to the quick.
"The way that ol' steer quit the country,
  he couldn't a been that sick."

ILLUSTRATION BY
MIKE CRAIG

ON THE EDGE OF COMMON SENSE | BY BAXTER BLACK

The Anvil and the Telephone Pole

Sometimes a cowboy will ride a good-lookin' bad horse for longer than it makes sense. This flawed thinking might have a more universal application; i.e., hangin' on to a pickup, dog or girlfriend long after they've bit you or konked out.

It's even worse when the injured party thinks he can make a good horse, dog or wife out of a pretty renegade.

Roy was a California cowboy and an experienced horseman. Out of respect, the boss had given him the big, fancy 3-year-old bay to use in his string. He was green-broke, cinchy, snorty and antsy, but he looked so good in his white stockings and star.

Within two weeks, he'd pitched Roy into the rocks and broken his arm. But he was a good-lookin' devil, so Roy turned him into the horse pasture while his arm healed. Every day, Roy would see the bay grazing or kickin' up his heels, livin' the life of Trigger. This injustice began to prey on Roy. He himself couldn't throw a saddle over a horse or cut his own chicken-fried steak. All he could do was hand things to the chore boy.

Still, Roy was a trainer at heart and believed he could gentle the young horse down. One afternoon, he caught the horse and, with the help of one of the boys, saddled him…not to ride, just to do some groundwork. Behind the hay shed was a dilapidated board corral that'd serve as a round pen. Roy, using a plastic whip, put the pony doin' circles. But the horse was so skittish he'd race away, then stop, whirl and generally act like he had iron fillings in his gyro compass. To steady his gait and add some drag, Roy decided to attach an anchor. He got the boys to bring the shoein' anvil out to the corral. He then tied it to the saddle on a 10-foot leash and cracked the whip!

The first thing Roy noticed was "an anvil is not near as heavy when it's off the ground!" The horse went racing around the pen, the anvil bouncing, whacking and whip-lashing behind the frightened beast! Big pieces of old board and rotten post filled the air like a wood chipper! It sounded like a 747 crashing in a redwood forest! Roy stood frozen in the center, plastic whip limp in his good arm, as the board corral disintegrated around him.

When the big bay left the corral, the stirrups were bangin' together over the top of his back, and the anvil was in midair! It took the boys an hour to saddle up and track him. They found him five miles down the road. He'd been subdued by a telephone pole. There were three dallys around the pole, and the anvil hung chest high.

Of course, the bay looked no worse for wear. He was pickin' at the weeds around the pole.

Roy, however, was another story. 🐎

THE COW BRUTE

Under the right conditions, a cow brute can actually increase its intellect to a kind of primitive, reptilian brain-stem level.

❝ In western movies the cow herd is part of the scenery, like pinto beans on the plate . . . ❞

Acowman is the way he is because he works with stock. It is what ties us to the Laplanders, Swahilis, Outbackers, and the sheepherders the angels found on the outskirts of Bethlehem on that special night.

In western movies the cow herd is part of the scenery, like pinto beans on the plate . . . essential but in the background. In real life cows are the reason cowboys exist. It's why we get up. It's what we do.

Much ado is made of becoming one with your horse. The nuance of touch, feel, voice and nudge. Tuning your horse's sensitivity to your every whim . . . or vice-versa.

SUBTLE is not a word commonly associated with COW. Nor is REASON, as in, "That new mama won't take her calf. I'm going to go reason with her . . . hand me the shovel!"

It is this bovine predictable unpredictability, their unexpected circus agility, and their primitive adherence to " . . . An eye for an eye, a tooth for a tooth, and a trample, hook and gore for a moment of inattention," that makes the cow brute the ideal third leg in this triumvirate stool of cowboy, horse and cow.

Columns in this section have the common thread of routine chores: calving, feeding, treating, breeding, and regular cow maintenance. It's what your life would be like if raising cattle was part of it. And, like so many things in real life, it ain't always pretty.

ON THE EDGE OF COMMON SENSE | BY BAXTER BLACK

A Cowboy Needs a Cow

A cowboy needs a bovine like a sailor needs a plank,
Like a blister needs a toehold, like a robber needs a bank.
A cowboy needs cow brute like a pack mule needs a crup,
Like a stuntman needs an actor, like a catcher needs a cup.

A cowboy, friends, without a cow is moon without the earth,
As macho and heroic as a whithpered lithper's curth.
See, cowboys need a doggie like Quasimodo needs a hunch,
Like a redneck needs a beer can just to have something to scrunch.

I say a cowboy needs a cow; they're joined at the hip.
Politicians and reporters have the same relationship.
Without each other to torment, they don't know where to start.
Like criminals and lawyers, you can't tell them apart!

So, to those who think I'm whining, that I'm pitiful and sad,
That I'm just another loser throwing good love after bad,
It's not all that one-sided, as I've learned in therapy,
'Cause my cow finally admitted that she really needed me.

On the Edge of Common Sense

By Baxter Black

The Cowboy Way

Illustration by J.P. Rankin

A GOOD COWBOY will go beyond the call of duty and even put himself in harm's way to help a suffering beast. Doug and Patty run a ranch in that big wide country in eastern New Mexico. Last spring they'd received several loads of cow-calf pairs. The weather was against 'em and the calves went to scourin'.

The cows were turned out in a big pasture. Treating the calves wasn't easy. The morning of the incident, their neighbor, Caleb, came to help. He was ridin' a big mule. They trailed through the cows and spotted a good-sized calf lookin' humped up. They watched for a minute and confirmed he was, in fact, afflicted. Doug eased up and dropped a lazy loop around his neck.

It is a strange but almost predictable occurrence that a calf, who appears to be on the edge of his last breath can suddenly become a dynamo of jackrabbit speed and mad-dog energy when suddenly caught with a rope.

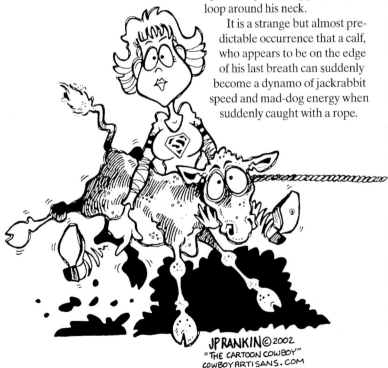

JP RANKIN © 2002
"THE CARTOON COWBOY"
COWBOYARTISANS.COM

Doug pulled the horn knot tight on his saddle as the calf slashed back and forth like a 200-pound marlin on the end of his line. Caleb was haulin' back on his mule to git outta the way. Not in time. The calf went around the outside of the mule and dang near toppled him before they jumped clear. The mule took off in high gear! Caleb was mashin' on the brakes. You could smell 'em burnin' as he disappeared over a swell.

Doug kept his pony facin' the calf 'till it tangled the rope in some brush.

"Quick, Patty," Doug instructed. "Flank him and give him a Sudafed and some L.A. 200!"

Patty, who's a good cowboy herself, dismounted, went down the rope and flanked the calf just as it's mamma arrived, registering her disapproval. She was blowin' snot as Patty maneuvered around tryin' to keep the calf between herself and mamma.

Doug saw Caleb out of his peripheral vision, racing back to the scene. "Great," he thought. "Help's on the way."

The mule was still out of control, on auto pilot, so to speak. He never slowed but jumped the stretched rope like a steeple-chaser. Caleb never shifted in his seat and disappeared out the other direction.

Patty had managed to give the shot and peel off the rope, but the cow gave her a good roll anyway before chasing off after her darlin' baby.

I was lookin' at Patty while Doug was tellin' me this story. She nodded with that resigned look I often see in ranch women's eyes.

I said, "By gosh, Doug. Yer a heck'uva cowboy. You did all that and never got off yer horse."

"Yup," he said, "I was trainin' him." 🐎

ON THE EDGE OF COMMON SENSE | BY BAXTER BLACK

The Fuzzy Slippers

ILLUSTRATION BY KEVIN CORDTZ

Some blamed the incident on her fuzzy slippers.

Brenda is a top hand and, like many ranch women, is especially good at calving heifers. Because of her skill and stamina, she and her husband, Perry, had synchronized 110 first-calf heifers to calve within a 2-week period. Of course, when they bred the heifers, they didn't anticipate those 2 weeks would fall in a period of clear skies and 40 degrees below zero.

Brenda kept two horses saddled in the barn, each on a 12-hour shift. She checked the heifer lot night and day, almost hourly, nipping back in the warm house for a bite or a nap. She'd slip off her cap, Carhartt coveralls and boots, then dive under the electric blanket. She slept in what she wore under the Carhartts, a T-shirt and underwear – "granny" underwear, she described it, Hanes Her Way, three in a pack for $2, which she got at Wal-Mart in Bismarck.

By the second week, Brenda was a zombie. During one particularly cold night she woke, dressed and walked to the corral. She noticed as she mounted her horse that she was still wearing her fuzzy pink slippers. "So what," her frozen jaw muscle mumbled.

Riding into the heifer lot, she found a new baby steaming in the frigid air. Brenda slid a loop around his hind legs, swung to the saddle and began skidding him across hard ground toward the calving jugs in the barn. Mamma followed. As Brenda passed through the gate, something went wrong. The calf's feet went to the inside of the post, the rope to the outside, snagging it in a perfect "V." It stopped the horse; he swiveled in his borium shoes to the left, snugged the rope up under his tail and threw a fit! Brenda pitched her slack, grabbed for the horn, reared back and pointed her fuzz-clad toes in a sort of "Michelin Man imitates Gjermunson."

The horse continued to buck as the 35-foot rope snaked itself free, steaming, writhing and throwing smoke from under the horse's tail, not unlike an 822-pound marlin, sounding and taking the line back from Ernest Hemmingway's whining reel!

Brenda came out over the front onto and into the ice, snow and frozen poop. She careened, luge-like into a snowbank, her fuzzy slippers disappearing and the handy openings on the side of the Carhartts packing with snow, from her grannys to her sockless ankles.

Back in the living room Perry was sympathetic, "He's never bucked before," he said, "It must've been the fuzzy slippers."

The following fall, one of the guilty slippers was found by a pheasant hunter in a coyote den 2 miles from the house. "Bet there's a story behind this," he thought, "bound to be." 🐴

On the Edge of Common Sense

By Baxter Black

A Bad Sign

The cow went down in the pasture.
　　I took it as a sign.
Like lightning striking my saddle horn
　　or guppies in the wine.

I'll have to pull the calf right here.
　　But it isn't raining hard.
It's just too bad that my slicker
　　is still back in the yard.

I taught my horse to ground-tie.
　　Like havin' an extra man.
Now why did he run off like that?
　　I really had a plan.

Thank goodness I've got a catch rope.
　　Whoa, darlin', just lay still . . .
You four-footed Double Whopper!
　　Your next stop is the grill.

Stay outta the blinkin' cattails!
　　At least they break the breeze.
For now she's stuck in the quagmire;
　　me, I'm up to my knees.

I've got both feet and I'm pullin'.
　　She's flat out on her side.
It's a water-cooled delivery.
　　He's comin' with the tide.

I feel like a scuba diver;
　　he hangs up at the hip.
I get his head on my shoulder;
　　it's hard to keep my grip.

He's slick as a newborn porpoise.
　　I heave him on the shore.
And plop, right there in the water,
　　just glad there ain't no more.

The cow, relieved of her burden,
　　rises outta the crud.
And walks the length of my body,
　　mashin' me into the mud.

My hat is the only thing floatin'.
　　I'm soaked from head to toe.
The cow is lickin' her baby
　　and watchin' me below.

I wait till he's up and suckin',
　　then slip out like a mouse.
And thank the Lord that I'm only
　　a half-mile from the house.

Illustration by Mad Jack Hanks

ON THE EDGE OF COMMON SENSE | BY BAXTER BLACK

The Taxidermy Heifer

As the only local cow vet, Steve had calved a lot of heifers
And as such was most reluctant to keep score
'Cause no matter how he tried and tried, he couldn't save
them all
So on the side he opened up a taxidermy store.

"Stuff yer heifer," was his motto, it was on his business cards.
And the message he recorded on the phone
Said, "If I can't save her, you can! As a conversation piece.
Have her mounted or just standing there alone."

He stuffed them in positions that he thought might catch the eye
One leg upraised, her milking on a tire
Or rearing up like Trigger, or with Xs on her eyes
Surrounded by a priest and candles waiting to expire.

There were action poses in the stance of how she last appeared
Like on her back, a huge midline incision
Or standing with the calf half out, a breech, the hind legs showing
That looked like some real bad rear-end collision.

Or head down in the charging mode, about to mow you down,
The water bag a timeless counterweight.
Or half a mount, just the backside, with your OB chains protruding
As you last saw her going out the gate.

His taxidermal specialty was a big C-section scar
The perfect touch to make the scene complete
Like his come-along calf-puller with a bow
in the pipe
Or glassy-eyed, a log chain 'round her feet.

The market for his heifers-in-distress grew leaps and bounds,
His cuddly cows kept flying out the doors.
People put them on the mantle, people placed them on
the lawn
Like pink flamingos grazing on all fours.

Until, alas, some thought they saw conflict going on
'tween his clinic and his taxidermy shop.
"These charges pain me deeply," he told his vet technician,
"My reputation's always been the top.

"What makes them think I'd compromise my veterinary work
To make a little money on the side?"
"Well, they might be misinterpreting your heifer calving
price," she said.
"Not many charge $5 and the hide."

On the Edge of Common Sense

By Baxter Black

Animal Bonding

Illustration by
J.P. Rankin

TODAY there is an increased recognition of the bonding process between man and animals. Pets are now referred to in politically correct circles as companion animals.

Companion—by definition, an associate, a comrade. It's not a bad choice of words in a world where families get fractioned, children leave home, neighbors don't know each other, and people get lonely. A pet can be a good companion.

Of course, when the word "bonding" is used, they are almost always speaking of the bonding between humans and dogs or cats. Wait … maybe not cats. I'm not sure one can bond with a cat. Unfortunately, I've seen some bonded to the highway out in front of my house.

But, be that as it may, they are never referring to livestock people and the animals in their care. Livestock bonding does occur infrequently in fiction. Babe, the sheepherding pig, bonded with Farmer Hoggett. Mary had her little lamb. Col. Sanders … well, that might be a bad example.

I contend that in real life, there is a bonding between stockmen and their creatures. I have got a lot of miles out of pickin' on cowmen who keep an old cow "one more year."

As a vet I have stood at the squeeze chute every fall as the cows are worked. My job is to give the cow a quick going over for physical fitness and do a pregnancy examination.

Typical deal: This ol' mama comes stumbling in the chute at the speed of a sloth on Valium. The headgate clangs shut, never touches the cow. Run a stick down her side, sounds like a prod pole across a picket fence. Her tail head is stickin' up like a shark's fin; she's draggin' one teat on the ground.

I'm thinkin' to myself, "Is there any point in putting on a plastic sleeve and torturing this pore beast any more?"

Then I look up to the headgate and there is that good cowman, rubbing his chin and lookin' at that old cow like he's in a jewelry store. "Am I missing something here?" I ask myself, dumbfounded.

I finally realized I was missing something. That good cowman and me were not looking at the same cow! See, I was looking at an economic unit. Will she have a calf, breed back, and bring another one home next fall?

He, on the other hand, was looking at an animal that had taken him to the pay window for 10 years. He might know her even better than that. She might have put him over a fence, or he might have helped her through a bad calving. But he knows her and owes her. He wants to make sure she gets the benefit of the doubt.

And that's a bond. As genuine as a cat or dog. Granted, he doesn't think of her as an associate or a comrade, as in "Git along little comrade," or "Let's go to the pasture and gather our associates." But it is a bond just the same, built on respect.

TOP PRODUCER

HIGHER PERFORMANCE

JP RANKIN © 2000
"THE CARTOON COWBOY"
CARTOON.COWBOY@HOTMAIL.COM

YOU MIGHT BE A COWBOY IF YOU'VE EVER CRIED AT THE CATTLE AUCTION.

On the Edge of Common Sense

By Baxter Black

Cattle-Handling Safety

Illustration by
Boots Reynolds

I TOOK part in the making of a video on cattle-handling safety put out by Oklahoma State University. It featured several experts including the well-respected cattle-handling expert Temple Grandin. The video stressed many recommendations that would seem like common sense—don't get in the crowding alley afoot, for instance.

I was pleased to be part of this fine effort, and I'm sure you can get a copy by calling 405-744-4050.

But when you consider the cowboy mentality, I might have added a few more guidelines that would appear self-explanatory to normal people. For instance:

Never tie the tail of your rope to your belt and then rope a cow.

Never lie down in the bottom of a crowding alley.

Never attempt to ride a cow out of a squeeze chute.

Never stand behind the sorting gate.

Never drink from a water trough wired with an electric heater that has three dead cows lying beside it.

Do not wear a mask and cape when flanking calves at a branding.

Do not grab the funny-shaped end of a branding iron.

Do not attempt to bulldog a steer by biting his nose as they let him out of the squeeze chute.

Do not try to remove a cud from a masticating bovine.

Never insist to the boss that you can pick up a bull's foot.

Avoid falling asleep while doing a rectal exam on a cow.

Do not straddle squeeze chute handles or small ruminants.

Don't stand too close to anyone with "doctor" in their name.

Never stick your hand between the sidebars of a squeeze chute when it's loaded with cow.

Do not lean against mammals.

Do not attempt to drive livestock with a bow and arrow.

And finally, steer clear of stuff labeled "DANGER," "CAUTION," or "COWBOYS AT WORK."

ON THE EDGE OF COMMON SENSE | BY BAXTER BLACK

Jack's Squeezeless Chute

Louise said, "When I heard the tractor start, I turned and came back in the house."

We'd worked Jack's calves with only one mishap. It involved a loose cinch, a big calf and a tall horse. When Jack hit the ground, it made waves in the water trough. I thought surely Louise would hear, but apparently she didn't.

"Could we take a look at that lump on No. 12's jaw?" Jack asked. He called her No. 12 because she had an ear tag with a 12 on it. I don't know what it signified because none of the other cows had tags. We cut her out and put her in the chute. Notice I didn't say squeeze chute.

In our neighborly cow community I do the odd veterinary procedure, Dick hauls the molasses, Pancho fixes the fence and Jack welds. Jack's chute was the result of many sleepless nights planning and plotting on how to build a cow-restraining device out of lengths of pipe, pieces of tin, chunks of chain and coffee cans of bolts that could be salvaged from his rusting bone yard.

His accomplishment was measured by how little expense was incurred and, possibly, the weight of the finished product. It actually looked quite sleek. The fact that it had no moving parts added to its intrigue, but when Jack opened, closed and folded nearby gates in a demonstration of cowboy origami, I began to see how it worked. It was a vision of efficiency.

We injected the cow into the top of the chute. She slid through the pipes like a gumball going down a waterslide. After that, everything happened so quickly. Just snatches of scenes remain in my mind: the cow sitting up and begging, a horn stuck through the side, one hind leg under the bottom pipe past the hock, ropes at various times around her horns, her rump and her hind leg.

During one frozen moment I was able to insert a needle into the lump and determine it was an abscess. When I looked back with a scalpel in hand to lance it, I had to go to the other side of the chute because she was now upside-down.

When I returned with some iodine for a final dousing, I had to reach above my head to complete the procedure. "All done!" I said, "Turn her out!"

Not a chance, she was wedged in like a thorn under King Kong's fingernail. We had to literally lift the chute off her so she could escape.

That must've been about the time Louise came out of the house to check on us and decided it was just a little too soon. 🐎

ON THE EDGE OF COMMON SENSE | BY BAXTER BLACK

Crazy Cow & Crazy Buck

Kevin bought the crazy cow at the Willcox sale. She was a big, black, hornless, part-Braymer with a red patch of hair on her poll like Woody Woodpecker.

That spring they planned to move a few of the cows in the gooseneck trailer to a far pasture. All but the crazy cow loaded. She ran to the back-side of the corral and paced the fence. The cowboy walked to the end of the corral to push her up. Kevin assumed a strategic spot to guide her in the right direction. She took off at a dead run. As she approached Kevin, she swerved and hit him full-speed, full-frontal!

According to onlookers, Kevin was thrown in the air, cartwheeled heli-copterally horizontal and was flung to the ground, unconscious. She walked him like a foot-log, crashed through the corral and disappeared into 11,000 acres.

Kevin was stabilized by his wife (a nurse, thank goodness), and airlifted to the hospital. He returned the next day the color of an eggplant, with countless stitches.

When they gathered cows the fol-lowing fall, Crazy was missing in action. "Maybe she was mistaken for a deer and shot by a hunter," Kevin speculated hopefully, but, alas, a phone call popped that bubble.

It was the forest ranger from the other side of the mountain 15 miles away. "I've got your cow," she said. "Lazy W cross, big black cow with a goofy looking red topknot. Yours, right?"

"Yeah," said Kevin. "I haven't seen her for months; she's crazy! I'll come and get her and take her straight to the auction!"

"Why, that must not be the same cow! This one's not crazy at all! Matter of fact, I'll buy her from you," said the ranger. "She saved my life! We had a crazy mule deer buck around here early fall. He came up on my lawn and attacked my dog. Had him pinned with his horns and was trying to eviscerate him with his hoofs. As I watched from the window, that cow came charging across the grass, hit the deer broad-side and chased him off!

"What's more, a week later I was out feeding the horses when I heard the sound of thundering hoofs. I looked over my shoulder, with a bucket in each of my hands, and saw that crazy deer coming right at me, head down, charging, just a breath away. In the microseconds it took for me to comprehend my sit-uation, out of the clear blue, from my blind side, came the crazy cow! She mowed that deer down like a freight train!"

Kevin was bumfuzzled. He accom-modated the ranger, but he still lies awake nights wondering what it was that he and the deer had in common. He still doesn't know, but as a precaution he's quit wearing his musk cologne. 🐴

ON THE EDGE OF COMMON SENSE | BY BAXTER BLACK

Wanda and the Wild Heifer

It was a cold, starry night somewhere in West River, Dakotaland. Calving had been under way a couple of weeks. Ed and Wanda were already into the heifer-checking routine.

On this particular night, Wanda had taken the middle-of-the-night duty. Ed had stayed up late trying to fix a water leak in the barn. Water pipes are buried deep up north. Ed had dug a hole big enough to bury a small mule. Grunt-work – frozen ground, mud under the permafrost. He located the break, shut off the main line and called it quits for the night.

After Wanda reheated supper for him, he hit the hay. It was midnight and he fell asleep, exhausted. Wanda set her alarm for 2:30 a.m. She'd make the deep-in-the-night heifer-check and let Ed rest. Ranch wives are the unsung work force in the glamorous panorama of the romantic life of the cowboy.

Imagine, if you will, instead of billboards depicting the handsome, macho Marlboro Man, you see a full-color spread of a red-faced woman with steamed-up glasses, wearing lumpy, well-used canvas coveralls, her nighty wadded up around her waist, poking out above the zipper, maybe a torn down jacket with dehorning blood on the sleeve, hair sticking out underneath a ratty wool stocking cap, mismatching gloves and muddy, slip-on, rubberized moon boots that look more like deer liver than clothing.

The alarm woke Wanda. She bundled up and stomped out to the barn. She moved one nervous heifer from the calving lot into the barn. The heifer didn't like the move and got on the fight. Wanda tried to bluff. It didn't work. The heifer charged! Wanda scrambled over the portable panels that composed the sides of the pen and fell...right into the hole Ed had dug earlier. The heifer tried to jump the panels after her but succeeded only in knocking one over – right on top of the hole, trapping Wanda underneath. Then, just when you were thinking, "Poor Wanda," the heifer landed feet-first on top of the panel, driving all four legs down through the bars.

Wanda lay flat of her back as four bovine, cloven hooves paddled furiously 12 inches above her frayed and frigid evening wear. It was like the fish-eye view of swimming cows. Four hours later Ed woke, shaved, made coffee and came out to the barn looking for the love of his life. 🐎

ON THE EDGE OF COMMON SENSE | BY BAXTER BLACK

Tilt Tables vs. Roping

KEVIN CORDTZ

Springtime. Grass is greenin' up, wildflowers are blooming, long johns are comin' off, and it's brandin' time! It's a festive occasion on lots of ranches. For years it's become a time for neighbors to get together and help one another.

The cows and calves have been gathered the day before. By daylight horses have been unloaded, everybody's saddled up and the calves are sorted from their mamas. In the corral, propane burners and branding pots are set up, brands heating, vaccine guns loaded, ear tags laid out, and dad's knife is sharp enough to clean a hornfly's fingernails!

Idyllic ... right?

Wait ... technology has reared its sleek, rancher's-helper-automated-finger-mashing-clanging-banging head, in the form of a tilt-table calf squeeze chute!

So nowadays, when your neighbor invites you to come help him brand his calves, you mumble around. You're feeling him out as to whether he's still roping them and draggin' them to the fire or pushing them through a long narrow alley, catching them in a calf chute and immobilizing the wiggling beasts. Sure, you appreciate that it's easier on the calves, the help and the horses, that it takes less time and labor, even less space than the traditional way, but it's so ... mechanical, so feedlot, so farmish. It's like work!

Branding calves isn't supposed to be work! It's supposed to be like Christmas! The Fourth of July! Going to the National Finals Rodeo! Not like getting your Army physical or helping your neighbor unload a semi full of salt blocks. You dress up to come to a branding. You wear your chaps and your spurs, not your coveralls and steel-toed Redwings. You worry about missing your dally, not banging your head.

Getting run over in the alley lacks the excitement of having a calf run under your horse. A deft jab with a Hot Shot or professional SQ injection doesn't elicit the same "Yee-haws" as a beautiful over-the-shoulder catch double-hocking a snaky calf.

It's the difference between shooting a pheasant out of the air or hitting one with your car. Besides, it gives your horse a purpose, and you a little glamour. And we can all use that now and then. 🐎

BAXTER BLACK

ON THE EDGE OF COMMON SENSE

Cow Disturber

Illustration by Ernie Franklin

McGRAW posed an interesting question. If a cowboy herds a herd of cattle, we call him a herder. If a sheepman herds a flock of sheep, he is still a herder. Why isn't he called a flocker?

Oley has always referred to himself as a cow molester. I think that is an accurate description of what cowboys do. The definition of molest is: to annoy or disturb.

"Where ya goin', Bill?"

"I'm gonna go check the cows." Which really means, "I'm gonna ride into the bunch, git 'em all up, turn 'em around, and just generally annoy and disturb them."

I grant there are occasions when we have a certain definite task in mind; i.e., "I'm gonna bring in that cow with the arrow in her side." Or, "Saddle up, we're pushin' 2,600 head of Longhorns to the sale in Bloomfield."

But most of the time we're just molesting them. Like doting parents or cat fanciers, we take any excuse to fuss over the critters in our care. It's a wonder white-tailed deer or jack rabbits aren't extinct with no one to molest them regularly.

If we were honest with ourselves, we would be more forthright.

The cattle foreman in the feedlot might give his instructions like this: "Jason, I want you to enter the first pen in the north alley. Unsettle the steers by sitting quietly for a moment. Next upset them by approaching. Confuse them by weaving back and forth, agitating and irritating them constantly. Badger each one until they've all gotten up and milled around. Once you're convinced you've stirred them up sufficiently, you may go molest the next pen."

Or, the cowman might say to his wife, "Darlin', while I'm at the board meeting I'd like you to torment the heifer in the barn lot every 20 minutes. She's tryin' to calve. Peek over the fence and disturb her. Shine the light in her eyes to break her concentration. Worry her as often as needed, and when I get back, I'll slip in and frighten her into calving."

In fairness, we are doing what all good shepherds do. We watch over our flocks because that is our calling. We stand guard in case any should need our help. But if truth-in-labeling is ever applied to our job descriptions, we will have to be more specific about what we do.

So the next time somebody asks what you do, try one of these on for size: herd rearranger, bull nudger, sheep panicker, mule cusser, equine perplexer, steer beautician, hog motivator, Holstein therapist, cow companion, dog shouter, or cowboy coddler.

On the Edge of Common Sense

By Baxter Black

Loose Cow Party

Illustration by Kevin Cordtz

"It's for you," his darlin' told him as he lay back in the chair
  For a well deserved siesta. Ugh, it wasn't really fair.
It was Chuck, his nearest neighbor—did he have to call right now?
  Millard took the phone and listened, "Are you sure that it's my cow?"

As if he'd changed his brand last week or something equally absurd
  Like the F.B.I. was posing as a member of his herd
Or an alien invasion took possession of his place
  And planned to infiltrate the earth as clones from outer space.

But no easy explanation seemed to ease his heavy load
  Chuck said, "Better come and get her, she's a'grazin' on the road."
Saddled up, he hit the highway and broke into a jog
  With his wife not far behind him in the pickup with the dog.

He could spot the cow's location from within a half a mile
  Cars were backed up to the corner, everybody wore a smile.
Helpful tourists waved and hollered, horsemen galloped to and fro
  Swingin' ropes like polo players, someone takin' video.

Millard rode into the melee as the cow turned up the lane.
  She trompled through the clothesline draggin' laundry like a train
Through the hogwire to the garden, through the hotwire to the corn,
  'Cross the rows with corn stalks flyin', laundry hangin' off her horn.

There were 15 mounted riders rattlin' through the stubble field,
  Millard got a rope around her but he knew his fate was sealed
When he felt the horn knot grabbin' and the saddle slip an inch . . .
  He remembered he'd forgotten to retighten up his cinch.

He was still there in the saddle but it now sat on the neck.
  We should pause and take reflection while we visualize the wreck. *(pause)*
Millard peeled off the equine like a dirty undershirt
  He was still tall in the saddle when his boot heels hit the dirt.

You could think of water skiing. You could think of Roto-Till
  But when 15 mounted riders mash you flat, it's all downhill
Millard watched from his position in the furrow that he'd plowed
  While the cow crashed through the hotwire, disappearin' in the crowd.

There the band of merry revelers in gesture grandiose
  Lashed up the draggin' rope somehow, around a solid post.
The crowd began to dissipate. It was over, they could sense
  Leavin' Millard to apologize to Chuck about his fence.

Chuck was gracious. Millard thanked him for his helpfulness and such
  But it seemed like Chuck enjoyed it . . . just a little bit too much.
But he really couldn't blame him. When a loose cow wreck occurs
  It's a miserable fiasco, less of course, it isn't yers!

ON THE EDGE OF COMMON SENSE | BY BAXTER BLACK

Fall: Cow-Workin' Time

It's fall. Cow-workin' time. Calf-shipping time. As the cowboy yearned for in song, "I'd like to be in Kansas for the roundup in the fall." Really it was Texas, for the roundup in the spring, but on most outfits fall is a bigger deal.

The whole point is to pull the calves off the cows, preg-check the cows, then ship the culls and the calf crop. It's payday. Harvest time. The reckoning.

Compared to the other big seasons in the cow business, i.e., branding, calving, turning out to summer pasture, or pulling the bulls, shipping time is the Super Bowl. Everyone's pumped up. Expectations are high – a year's work. It's like adding up your score at the end of the game. Most businesses accumulate income daily or weekly. But on a ranch, the only things you accumulate regularly are bills. Christmas comes in the fall for cowmen.

The fall gather is often simple on an Ohio farm, where you might run two cows to the acre. Shake a grain bucket or take the dog and grandchild out on the four-wheeler and bring 'em back. But on a ranch that runs 400 cows on 20 sections, the gather often requires two or three days, bad weather, the banker, horseshoer, brother who lives in the city, all the kids and everybody's dogs to bring in the bunch.

The fall ranch gather is the height of rancher satisfaction: cool sunshine, crisp nights, autumn leaves, frisky calves, long days in the saddle, time to be proud of your horse, your kids, your way of life and your contribution to society. It's a time of thankfulness shared by corn farmers in the fall piloting their spaceships down the rows during the harvest, a high-school graduate listening to her commencement speaker, a cabinetmaker surveying his finished product hanging on the kitchen wall or a soldier come home after serving his tour of duty. It's a sense of fulfillment.

It's also the calm before the storm! Once they reach the home corrals, the calves are separated from their mammas and often sorted by sex and weighed. The bawling is deafening! Big semis arrive. Calves are loaded aboard and sent off to sale barns, feedlots or grass operations.

The cows are dry-lotted overnight and worked the next day. During their 30- to 60- second stop in the squeeze chute, each cow is given a quick examination; her teeth are checked to determine age, her eyes are checked (each cow is asked to read an eye chart), as are her feet and udders. The veterinarian does a rectal palpation to determine pregnancy.

If she's deemed healthy, bred and young enough, she's given vaccinations, vitamin A and a paraciticide and considered a keeper. At the conclusion of the rattling and banging and bawling and occasional outburst of sailor language, the cull cows are shipped, the good cows put in the meadow and everybody thanked. Then, when the dust has settled, there's usually time for football, fixing machinery, Christmas and kid's activities, and feeding cows.

Until calving season begins early next spring and the cycle starts again. 🐎

ON THE EDGE OF COMMON SENSE | BY BAXTER BLACK

Cowboy Emergency Room

It hasn't been a good year when the nurses in the emergency room call you by your first name. As in, "Roll on in here, Lee. What did ya do this time?"

Judy was talking to her grown daughter on the phone Sunday morning. "Yep, I'm finally talking your father into going to the hospital. He's in the bedroom tryin' to get his shirt on over the bad shoulder. Just a minute, I can't hear ya over his groanin'. Let me just close the bedroom door."

It began slowly and built till Lee finally had said, "I can't sleep on my left side 'cause of my bad arm, my right side 'cause

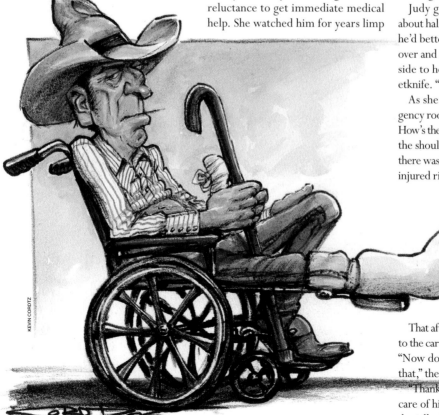

of my bad leg, or my back 'cause of my bad back." She traded him the recliner for the bed. The shoulder had been the accumulated erosion and "stalagazation" of buckin' hay, preg-checking cows and roping. He actually started wearing button-up undershirts since he couldn't raise his arm above his head. That worked until he broke his thumb in a hitchhiking accident and couldn't button his shirt.

"I'll get the shoulder fixed some day," he told the emergency-room doctor as they were taping his thumb. He repeated the commitment two months later as they were recasting the rebroken thumb.

Judy had always been resigned to his reluctance to get immediate medical help. She watched him for years limp

and bang around the house always waiting "one more day to see how it does." Her friends often lectured her about taking better care of him. She reminded them that there were rare occasions when she whisked him right to the emergency room in Steamboat, an hour away. Those were the two times he'd been unconscious.

"He hurt his ankle this morning tryin' to rope a sick calf," Judy continued explaining to her daughter. "The corral was icy, the horse went down. He went ahead and finished checkin' the new calves. Now he can't get his boot off. I better go help him. Bye, love ya."

Judy got Lee loaded in the car, but about halfway to Steamboat, he decided he'd better cut off the boot. She pulled over and came around to the passenger side to help. He handed her his pocketknife. "It's sharp," he said. "Yeoww!"

As she wheeled him into the emergency room, everybody said, "Hey Lee! How's the thumb? How's the knee? How's the shoulder?" Judy had to explain why there was blood and a knife wound in the injured right ankle. They were going to sedate him and had some official questions. "Does he have a church affiliation?"

She replied, "If we were religious, we'da been in church this morning, and this never woulda happened."

That afternoon, they wheeled him out to the car with his ankle tightly wrapped. "Now don't let him put any weight on that," they told her.

"Thanks for everything, I'll take good care of him!" she promised as she accidentally shut the door on his foot! 🐎

On The Edge Of Common Sense

By Baxter Black, D.V.M.

Eat More Beef!

Illustration by Boots Reynolds

I'm a fairly frequent victim of the EAT MORE BEEF! campaign.
  I've read the ads and seen the spots intended to explain
That if I will eat real beef, I will be real people
  And have more iron inside me than a rusty Army Jeep'll!

It will make me thin and happy and put my life in order
  And I agree in principle, I've been a staunch supporter.
But sometimes all this hoopla just plain gives me the jitters.
  See, I have a vested interest. I raise the blasted critters!

Which tends to make me cynical, to doubt or even scoff it!
  'Cause from a cowman's point of view, it ain't all fun and profit.
They've crippled more than one good horse and countless good blue heelers,
  An order buyer now and then, plus hordes of wheeler-dealers!

And as for me, I've had my share of wounds and lacerations,
  Of broken heads and swollen thumbs, unwelcome perforations.
They've knocked me down and knocked me out and overhauled my keister,
  And woke me up on Christmas Day and kept me up till Easter!

They've embarrassed and ignored me, annoyed and misused me.
  They've broke me flat as hammered pie, mistreated and abused me.
And yet I keep on comin' back like bees keep makin' honey.
  Maybe I'm a masochist 'cause it dang sure ain't the money!

So when they tell me EAT MORE BEEF!, I'll try and be attentive.
  But tellin' me's a waste of time, I've got my own incentive.
I've spent a lifetime workin' cows, which keeps a man believin'.
  You bet yer life I EAT MORE BEEF! . . . I eat it to get even!

On the Edge
of Common Sense

By Baxter Black

Feedlot
Heroes

NOW AND then I get to thinkin' I should quit this feedlot job.
  Go and ride with Buster, what's his name, his Texas wagon mob.
Maybe move to old Montana, wear them bat wings for a while
  Or do California day work in the old vaquero style.

I get my western magazines, shoot, I keep 'em by my chair
  And I read 'em after lunchin', sometimes wishin' I was there.
See, it all looks so romantic. All they do is brand and ride
  Maybe gather up some wild ones, push 'em down the other side

While the cameras keep on snappin', set against a scenic view
  Lookin' picturesque and western, quintessential buckaroo.
It's not often that reporters come by here and spend a day
  And the stories that they usually write are mostly exposé

And I really can't remember any artist incidents.
  All the painters that I've ever seen were workin' on the fence.
'Cause nobody wants to see us cowboys dressed in overshoes
  In our insulated covies on a feedlot winter cruise,

Sortin' fats in some bleak alley with the mud up to our knees,
  Shovelin' bunks or treatin' sick ones, fightin' flies or allergies.
I take a little nap sometimes, in my chair there after lunch
  And I dream that I am workin' for some rope and ride 'em bunch

Where a roaming photo graffer lookin' for the real thing
  Is dazzled by my cowboyness, the essence of my being.
And he poses me majestic by the River Babylon
  Mounted on my paint caballo, conchas glistening in the sun.

But at five till one I waken with the image in my mind
  Of the picture he has taken for the cover, but I find
I'm portrayed in all my glory standin' in the chronic pen
  Lookin' at a scruffy lump jaw that needs lancin' once again.

I get up and grab my jacket that's the color of manure
  And I head back to the feedlot, catch some horses for the shoer,
But I worry if my heroes in that cowboy magazine
  Ever get a lick of work done, 'cause they always look so clean.

Illustration by Mike Craig

On the edge of common sense

By Baxter Black

Medical or nutritional

ONE OF the most important traits of a good feedlot manager is the ability to assign blame. That is the reason they often employ consulting vets and nutritionists. It keeps them from having to fire regular employees.

Unfortunately, it also pits the veterinarian against the nutritionist in their everlasting battle to decide whether a problem is nutritional or medical.

The feedlot manager sat across the desk from his *Nutritionist of the Month* and his *Vet de Jour*. He spoke, "I've been looking at our death loss records and we've had a lot of bloats this month."

"Obviously nutritional," interjected the vet, who sat back, relieved.

"Now let's not jump to conclusions," said Nute. "I just read an article in the *Academy of Sciences Journal* where they suspect an esophageal thickening in mastodons during the last ice age that could lead to interference with

Illustration by Kevin Cordtz

normal rumen gas elimination, thus contributing to an increase in bloat. And you know it's been a cool autumn."

"What?" said the vet.

Nute continued, "And not only that, you are aware that sudden decreases in atmospheric pressure may increase the gas pressure inside the rumen. I've been keeping daily records of the barometric pressure, which proves my point."

The manager wiped his eyes. "In addition, we're losing more weaners than normal to pneumonia this fall."

"Obviously medical," said the nutritionist, glad to be out of the hot seat.

"Well, yes," admitted the vet, "but I've not been able to culture any unusual organisms out of the lungs, so they should be responding to our treatment. But they aren't, which leads me to believe it could be something in the hay or possibly the supplement that is the initial causative agent. Maybe a mineral deficiency or ration imbalance."

"What?" said the nutritionist.

Merlin, the vet, continued. "Plus the original insult may be the result of calves breathing ammonium fertilizer."

"Well, I'm breathing a lot of fertilizer in this room," said the manager. "How 'bout the increasing incidence of brainers?"

"Hemophilus," said Nute.

"Thiamine deficiency," said the vet.

"Bad eyes?" asked the manager.

"Wheat chaff," said the vet.

"Viral," said the nutritionist.

"I give up," gasped the manager. "Oh, I see we had one die from trauma. He was hit by a feed truck."

"Definitely nutritional," said the vet.

"Yes, but as I recall," said Nute, "they ran over him in the sick pen."

ON THE EDGE OF COMMON SENSE | BY BAXTER BLACK

Every Cowman's Nightmare

It was every cowman's nightmare.

Owen's ranch in Globe, Ariz., was a long way from the Prescott sale barn. Getting there also involved passing through the "Gates of Hell," as Owen referred to the booming, seething expanse of asphalt and dragon's breath called Phoenix. Girding his loins, he loaded one old bull and 10 cull cows in his 20-foot gooseneck trailer and came down the mountain. Even at 5 p.m. on that hot summer evening it was well above 100 degrees Fahrenheit.

Of course, he planned on reaching Phoenix so he could be part of the after-work traffic. Even with five lanes on his side of the freeway, it was like suddenly finding yourself wearing a sail in a windstorm. Owen gripped the steering wheel as he squinted into the blinding sun. Cars roared around him, big trucks rocked his long-bed four-by-four as they whizzed by. The noise was overwhelming.

WHAM! THUMP! The steering wheel jerked in his hand! Cars honked and swerved away to his left! His good dog was pounding on the back window and pointing! Owen's first thought was that someone had hit him from behind. Then he looked in his side-view mirrors. Black smoke, bull manure, pieces of rubber and a rooster-tail of sparks flew out from under the right side of his trailer! The whole rig dragged to a stop like someone had thrown an anchor overboard. The dog was covering his eyes.

Gouging his way to the shoulder, Owen stopped the crippled conveyance. "A blowout," he was thinking, glad he'd checked the spare before leaving the ranch. Imagine his disappointment when he noticed there were two. Blowouts, I mean, on the same side. And not enough room to get a jack under the trailer and no hump to pull up on.

Dusk fell on the cowboy. The temperature on his side of the freeway dropped to 98 degrees as he sat pondering his dilemma, Should he unhook? Leave the loaded trailer? Kick the dog? Set the cattle free? Quit ranching? Blame his wife?

An hour into the pondering, when he was actually considering such solutions as joining the National Guard or learning the art of western pottery, help arrived. Owen and the Good Samaritan did some additional pondering. The Good Samaritan drove back to his house and returned with a large piece of concrete. They placed it in front of the bare right front rim and managed to pull the fully loaded trailer up on top of it. It raised the trailer high enough to allow one spare to be affixed.

The Good Samaritan would accept no money. Owen gave him a Cowbelle's placemat that included his ranch brand, and his effusive thanks. It was midnight when he finally pulled back on the road. The temperature had dropped to 92 degrees. 🐎

KEVIN CORDTZ

ON THE EDGE OF COMMON SENSE | BY BAXTER BLACK

Feeding Cows Flint-Hills Style

ILLUSTRATION BY KEVIN CORDTZ

Feedin' the cows in the wintertime has a romantic side. The calendar picture is of two Belgians pullin' a hay sled through knee-deep snow, pine-clad mountains, blue sky, puffy clouds, leavin' a trail of bright green hay, pied-pipering fat cows in its wake.

There are regional versions. In the Midwest substitute tractors for horses, in Jackson Hole substitute elk for cows, in Lubbock substitute gin trash for hay, and in Arkansas substitute mud for snow.

But it's a good time in the cow business. The weaners are long since shipped, the loan is renewed, the cows are heavy with calf, and we're waitin' for the cycle to begin again.

Ronnie ran a small set of cows on the edge of the Flint Hills. One beautiful Kansas mornin', he loaded six bales of hay on the back of his 1-ton flatbed, took the dog and puttered out to the pasture. Though the sun was shining, the high ground was white with frost. The bogs and low spots reflected the sun's rays like mirrors.

Both of Ronnie's knees were bad. To avoid the constant stopping, starting, bending and climbing, he treated his 225-horsepower turbo-diesel dually like a one-horse sleigh. By placing the transmission in compound-low, it'd crawl no faster than he could walk. He could make one leap up to the bed, break bales and scatter hay as his pickup wound its way on autopilot across the pasture at a leisurely pace.

He was thus engaged, when he dropped his twin cutting knife. He quickly put his foot onto the trailer hitch and stepped off the moving vehicle. Ronnie easily could've retrieved his knife and caught up if fate had not intervened, but he slipped on the hitch and the 2-inch chrome ball caught underneath his jeans cuff!

He hopped along behind on one bad knee the length of a coffin, then folded into the shape of a pointed finger. Although the grass was smooth, the journey did include the low spots and occasional hedgerow.

The neighbor who eventually rescued Ronnie said that from a distance Ronnie looked like someone trolling for largemouth bass.

Thankfully, it came out okay in the end. Ronnie eventually had both knees replaced. But he still tells the story, and always finishes by saying, what with the dog barking and the cows mooing, he could hardly hear himself cuss! 🐎

On the Edge of Common Sense

By Baxter Black

If Herefords Were Black

I f Herefords were black and Angus were red
    would breeders of Herefords breed Angus instead?
I mean, would the people who bred Angus first
    be now breeding Angus if things were reversed?

Or would they be loyal to red, white, and true
    to color of cowlick be always true blue?
If such were the case would they dis all the blacks,
    tell jokes about prolapse, compare them to yaks.

More suited for saddle or wearin a yoke
    than stubbornly breeding until they go broke.
And those of the Aberdeen Angus cartel
    would they tout maternal endowments, as well,

Promoting their native resistance to thorns,
    while cursing as mutants those not sprouting horns.
Just draggin' their sheath through the cheatgrass and burrs
    like leaky ol' bass boats nobody insures.

Illustration by Don Gill

Debate would rage on like it does anyway
    if South had worn blue or the North had worn gray,
Or if Henry Ford had been Hank Chevrolet
    you'd still be a Ford man . . . or would you, today?

So if Herefords were black and Angus were red
    would breeders of Herefords breed Angus instead?
The question begs deep philosophical thought
    but don't get disgruntled or get overwrought.

The breeders of purebreds run true to the grain
    and efforts to change them would just be in vain.
And not 'cause they think other cattle are bad—
    "I'm stickin' with this one, 'cause that's what Dad had."

ON THE EDGE OF COMMON SENSE | BY BAXTER BLACK

The Round-Bale Feeder

The mechanical genius of man has been modifying hay feeders since Jacob's father-in-law invented baling twine. This is due to the bovine ability to ravage, scatter and tromp more hay than it ever could eat. Even today, feeding hay on the ground can be written off as bedding.

The round-bale feeder has gained popularity for reducing waste. Without it, dumping an 800-pound round bale naked in the middle of a corral is akin to throwing a meatloaf into a sinkful of piranhas.

Chuck has used these feeders the last few years. They're 8 feet in diameter with a solid side that encircles the ring like a 2-foot-wide hatband. The vertical bars rise another 24 inches and connect to the top ring and are spaced to allow one cow per space to stick her head through. Then you dump your hay inside the ring and, *voilá!*

One late, very cold winter afternoon, Chuck drove out to feed. He had 20 bales of alfalfa on the back of his 1-ton flatbed.

He noticed the feeder wasn't where it'd been that morning. He was pondering how it'd been moved, when one of his good cows stuck her head through the bars in anticipation. Using the cow logic she'd used since birth – i.e., if a head will pass through a hole, surely a body will – she pressed on, getting both front feet inside the ring, and became stuck. The feeder tipped up till it looked like she was wearing a galvanized hoop skirt.

Using his cow logic, Chuck stepped onto the opposite side of the ring, thinking his weight and encouragement would free her. He quickly learned how the feeder had been relocated.

Off they went across the frozen Kentucky tundra like a dog team! Chuck had been to a county fair, was a volunteer fireman and had gotten hung up in the O.B. chains once, but he'd never had a ride like this!

He swerved, swung, pounded, bounced, banged and bonged like a chicken tied behind a dirt bike. Each piercing scream increased the cow's velocity!

Thanks to the growing darkness, neither Chuck nor the cow saw the ravine. They were airborne for what seemed an eternity. The cow sailed front feet first and speared into the opposite muddy bank. The sudden stop dislodged the feeder, but not before it sling-shotted Chuck, fence pliers over tea kettle, into briars on the other side! He racheted to a scratchy stop.

The cow staggered off, and Chuck slogged back to his rig to try and retrieve the feeder. After seeing that his other cows and one horse had managed to savage and scatter all the bales off his flatbed, not to mention turning his down jacket into cud, he decided it could wait till morning.

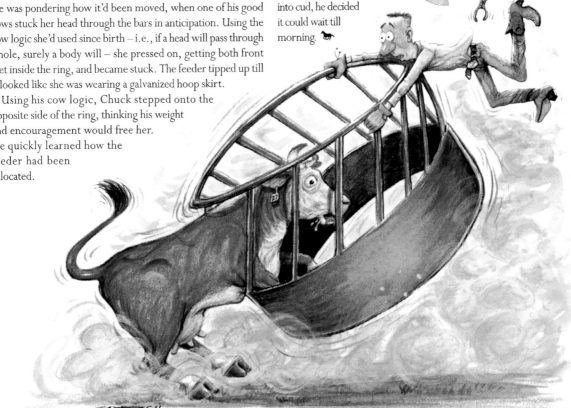

ON THE EDGE OF COMMON SENSE | BY BAXTER BLACK

Buffalo Trading

The lure to own something of historical significance is strong — Benjamin Franklin's signature, an arrowhead, Dale Evan's Chapstick®. This connection to tradition is part of the popularity of raising buffalo, I think. However, putting bison on display on your farm is more "complicated" than parking an antique tractor in your shed.

Kenny was having a clearance sale. Four buffalo cows and one bull. A country gentleman with 20 acres called, and a deal was made. The gentleman assured Kenny he knew what he was doing. His wife and he already had two llamas and an emu, and he'd seen *Dances With Wolves*.

He showed up at Kenny's place in a brand-new Chevy ¾-ton pickup and a 20-foot stock trailer that didn't have a scratch or speck of manure on it. Kenny's own buffalo-hauling trailer looked more like an armored car or the bed of a dump truck. He looked at the ¾-inch pipe and tin-foil sides of the gentleman's rig and decided to keep his mouth shut. It took the gentleman 30 minutes and 40 acres to get backed up to the loading chute. He walked back wearing his brand-new black cowboy hat, boots and a buffalo-head bolo tie, carrying a bullwhip.

"What do I do?" he asked.

"Sit in the pickup till I get 'em loaded," said Kenny.

The cows complied, but the bull was being difficult. Finally, Kenny got him to where he was sniffing the trailer floor when the gentleman poked his head around the corner, spooking the bull and causing Kenny to dive for cover!

After reinstructing the gentleman to stay in the truck, Kenny snapped a long lead rope to a chain that hung from a ring in the bull's nose. Kenny then ran the lead rope around a pipe in the trailer, took a dally on a corral

post and worked the bull back up the chute, right to the trailer again. Once again, in an effort to help, the gentleman peered around the corner, scaring the bull who pulled back so hard the snap broke! The lead rope whipped around, the broken snap cracked across the gentleman and broke his arm!

"What do I do?" cried the gentleman.

"Stay in the truck!"

The third time was the charm; the bull loaded with a little help from a plastic bag and a fence stay. He circled and banged inside his cage while the gentleman counted out the cash with his good arm. Suddenly the bull charged the tailgate, got a horn under one horizontal bar and ripped three of them loose! The welds popped like snaps on a shirt! He stuck his head out.

"What do I do?" hollered the gentleman.

"They're not mine," said Kenny to the gentleman behind the wheel. "But I believe 'bout every couple of minutes I'd slam on the brakes to keep him from makin' the hole bigger."

Kenny watched as the truck and trailer headed down his driveway with the buffalo stickin' out like a trophy on the den wall. Then he heard the screech of brakes and saw the buffalo disappear!

Tradition don't come easy.

On the Edge of Common Sense

By Baxter Black

Trolling for Buffalo

Buffalo Bob took the call on his cellular phone. I caught the last of the conversation . . . "and if that don't work, try a shot. No . . . not a tranquilizer, a 30-30. At least you'll be able to eat the meat.

"Escaped buffalo pose a problem," he said after hangin' up. "That fellow was callin' from West Virginia. I told him a trick that worked for me . . . trolling."

Bob explained that a few years back he and Dave bought 12 head of buffalo from a grain farmer on the plains of Colorado. Bought 'em over the phone. The price was right.

They arrived in the small town of Flagler and took a motel room. Three days later they were still tryin' to gather the 12 head.

The first day they built a trap out of panels in the quarter-section pasture. The trap was big enough to fit the USS Eisenhower. They

Illustration by Kevin Cordtz

baited it with alfalfa and spent all afternoon tryin' to coax, drive, and trick the suspicious buffalo herd into the trap. They ignored it like fat trout in a well-fished stream.

That night they called a noted wildlife veterinarian who had buffalo experience. The vet arrived the next day armed with a tranquilizer gun and enough ammo to put Yellowstone Park to sleep for a fortnight.

They drove out to the herd and re-enacted the stampede from *Dances With Wolves,* but hit nary a buffalo.

Concerned with the expense of the tranquilizer, Bob and Dave built a buffalo blind outta tumbleweeds. They parked the vet with his trusty musket behind the tumbleweeds and chased buffalo by him for 2 hours. Unfortunately "Dr. Dead Eye" couldn't hit the top of his head with a chafing dish. Not one bullseye.

The third morning found Bob and Dave making excuses to the grain farmer. "Well," he said, "do what you can. They're yours. I've got to go to Dad's place and haul a dead calf to the dump."

A light flickered somewhere in Buffalo Bob's desperate brain. He remembered tryin' to drag a dead buffalo calf out of a field. The herd went crazy and followed the calf through some primitive protective instinct. He actually had to get the tractor into 4th high to stay ahead and get out of the gate!

"Bring that dead calf over here. I want to try somethin'."

The farmer complied, even though it was a Hereford cross.

Bob stationed a man by the trap gate and circled the herd draggin' the dead calf behind his pick-up. The buffalo cows went berserk and started chasin' the calf. Bob made a couple more circles stirrin' 'em up and on the third pass drove straight into the trap. The herd followed like greyhounds chasin' the mechanical rabbit!

"Wow!" I said, as the light dawned, "Trolling for buffalo. So that's what you advised your caller from West Virginia."

"Yeah. I don't know if it'll work, though," said Bob. "His buffalo is loose in a lady's back yard on the nice side of town."

THE ESSENCE OF EQUINE ETHOS

The horse person: someone who can look at a day-old
colt one time and pick that sucker outta the string 12 years later!

This little section actually represents a huge part of the horse industry worldwide, i.e., horses without cows. A horse person as opposed to cowboy. The Spanish word for horse person is so much more glamorous . . . *caballero*, which also translates to *gentleman*.

The leaning toward teaching horses good behavior gently is the key to the popularity of the boom in horse training clinics. It is not necessary for horses to be able to perform "practical" tasks. It is justification enough to teach the horse to be good for goodness' sake.

The horse people who own horses for the pleasure of riding are one of the biggest sources of revenue for trainers, veterinarians, hay brokers, saddle and tack sales, horseshoers, and special ingredient dealers.

It is also the group wherein most young horsemen and women get their first glimpse into the equine mind. And experience the beginning of the joy, the responsibility and the sadness that comes with having horses as a part of your life.

The first two or three years of my veterinary profession was a crash course in Horses vs. People. How to win them over, what makes them tick, and what it will take for a 1,200-pound, three year old stallion with rollers in his nostrils and fear in his eyes, to allow me to pass a hose through his nose and down to his stomach without getting killed.

I mastered that ability as well as others, but like most horsemanship skills, any good horseman will tell you, it can't be learned from a book.

On the Edge of Common Sense

By Baxter Black

Just a Girl and Her Horse

Illustration by
Don Gill

PAM AND JOE had a long-term relationship. She was a backyard horse person with a demanding day job, and he was a sorrel gelding that heard her innermost thoughts.

She had returned from the doctor's office, still woozy with sedative. She and her husband walked out into the sunset backyard to enjoy their Colorado front range mountain view. They immediately noticed ol' Joe at the far backside of the big pasture. Things did not look right.

"Go check him, hon," Pam asked Hubby, a little worried about her sorrel friend. Hubby soon sprinted back shouting, "Get the wire cutters and call the vet!"

Pam frantically called the vet. The numbers and buttons were weaving kaleidoscopically in her still foggy conscience.

"You've got to come, Dr. Jim! It's Joe! He's been hung in the wire … bleeding … don't know … please hurry!"

Hubby extricated Joe and led him down to the lot. Pam held the flashlight for Doc when he arrived. It turned out the wound was not serious. Doc bandaged him and administered antibiotics.

"He's acting funny," Pam kept saying, "He's antsy and he's got white circles around his eyes." They led Joe into the barn and stalled him. He snorted and circled.

"Look at his feet!" she exclaimed, "He's pulled his shoes off in the wire!" She ran in the house and called her horseshoer.

"Can't it wait 'till morning?" he asked.

At the dawn shoeing Joe had settled down somewhat, but he fought the shoer and hadn't eaten any of the apples Pam had left for him. Over the next three days, they got the pasture fence repaired and changed Joe's bandage but Pam continued to worry that he was not his old self yet.

Thursday night Pam answered a knock on her door. It was a large man who introduced himself as their back-pasture neighbor.

"I'm missin' a horse, have ya seen one?" he asked.

"Only mine," Pam explained. "He's down in the barn recuperating."

"Could I have a look?" the neighbor inquired. Pam bristled, "You think I don't know my own horse! I've had him over 10 years, he eats apples out of my hand! He's part of the family!"

"Does he have a brand?" asked the neighbor.

"Of course not! I'd never do that! Come look for yourself," she said with indignant assurance.

An hour later, as she watched the neighbor drive off, trailer in tow, hauling his bandaged, vetted, newly shod (for the first time, she had learned) sorrel mare, many unanswered questions became clear. Particularly the horse at the far side of the pasture, on the backside of the fence, that had been whinnying plaintively since Joe had been injured.

Pam is still trying to spread the blame around to Hubby, to Doc and to the horseshoer, but she knows the truth … and so does Joe. 🐎

ON THE EDGE OF COMMON SENSE | BY BAXTER BLACK

The Equine Ego

I was in a western store when a gentleman stepped up to the counter and asked me which cap that he was holding looked better. I asked if he was a baseball player, a member of a rap group or a corn farmer. He said none of the above, he was a horseman. I said,

"Follow me," and escorted him to the man behind the bench, shaping hats.

"Please show this fine pilgrim how he looks in a cowboy hat," I requested of the hat man. The buyer protested. I explained that wearing a good hat was a matter of pride. He said modestly, "Well,

I'm not a very good cowboy, I just own a couple of horses. A cap is good enough for me." "I didn't mean *your* pride," I explained, "I meant the horse's!"

Horses are dignified animals. Lookin' good is one of the things they do well, and they know it. You don't see many horses in casual wear by choice. Unlike most other animals, they have majestic ancestors as role models. They are the creatures of which legends are made. Can you think of another animal who could have been substituted to save the day for *The Man from Snowy River, The Lone Ranger,* Coronado, Robert E. Lee, Sir Lancelot or Sitting Bull?

No, they've tried camels, donkeys, elephants, even ostriches; unfortunately these beasts usually wind up as comic sidekicks. But when a hero needs a ride, he rides a horse. Pegasus, Sea Biscuit, Fury, Traveler, Champion, Trigger, Silver and Midnight. And the horse is expected to live up to this grand image. These expectations explain the quirks in horses' personalities; stubbornness, stupid habits, flightiness, overeating. They are insecure and must constantly be reassured.

Brushing, new shoes, nice tack, riders with good taste. The whole western-wear industry of designer saddles and brand-name jeans is fabricated to make the horse look good.

So, for my shabby horseman friend who didn't think he was qualified to "dress the part" by wearing a real hat, you can see the damage he might do to his horse's self-esteem.

It's like putting the bridle on over the halter. Do you think the horse doesn't notice? It's like wearing your underwear outside your pants.

So do your part, good horseman, remember, in riding, just like in cooking, presentation is half the meal. 🐎

ILLUSTRATION BY KEVIN CORDTZ

ON THE EDGE OF COMMON SENSE | BY BAXTER BLACK

Improving My Horsemanship

I consider myself as progressive as any horseman when it comes to considering techniques and devices for improving my horse's welfare or my horsemanship. Horse magazines are packed with testimonials and advertisements for all manner of horse improvement—supplies, seminars and secrets.

As I read the ad copy, including bold print like, "comfort, safety and style," "the world's largest," "tested and proven" or "the best ever made!" I am reminded that humans have been riding horses for millennia, and everything we take for granted today was once the brainstorm of some Mongolian or jolly old English knight's trainer.

"I don't know, Cedric When I heft my lance, it pulls me over and I fall off."

"Funny, Sir Lancelot, I was just reading, in the *Camelot Horseman*, about a new piece of gear invented by a team roper in western Wales called a 'steer up. I'll check into it."

You'd think, after centuries of marketing geniuses trying to sell a horseman one more thing, that we would have run out of ideas. I must have 25 different versions of hoof picks lying around: homemade, artistic, crude, sharp, shiny, worthless, fancy, and functional and farrier-approved.

I recently ordered a "cow paralyzer." That's not the trade name, but I'm going to avoid using trade names since there might be more than one company selling these devices. I'm anxious to try it on horses. They didn't guarantee it for horses, but I can imagine many circumstances when "a twitch is not enough."

I've bought stirrup swivels, knot elim-

inators, metal hondas, automatic gate openers, sweat-less saddle pads, fly masks, cribbing devices, fence climbers, freeze brands, magic minerals and special secret supplements.

My latest is, "a unique hoof-support system for the farrier horse owner and veterinarian," which is a lightweight fiberglass unit with an interchangeable foot cradle and straight post. It has magnets to hold rasps, nippers, clinchers, etc.

Actually, I like it! It replaces three "hoof-support systems" I'm using now, that are made of disc blades, two-inch pipe, tire tread and cotter keys, each system weighing more than a good-sized mastiff!

At a fair in Kanab, I bought a patented stirrup extender for my neighbor Jack. He's got a little age and is not of tall stature, so mounting involves parking his horse next to a cut bank, water trough or hay bale. We installed the stirrup extender on his saddle, which lowers the left stirrup a full three inches "with a push of the button."

Three days later, I asked Jack how his new stirrup extender was working.

"Great," he said. "But there's one complication. I can get my foot in the stirrup okay, but when I try to swing my leg over the saddle, I fork too soon!" 🐎

On the Edge of Common Sense

By Baxter Black

Pleasure Horses

I CONSIDER myself a former horse mechanic. The horses I did veterinary work on were ranch and feedlot beasts of burden. Workin' animals from man's point of view.

Up until about 50 years ago that would describe most of the horses vets worked on. I was always a little vain about distinguishing that *my* patients worked for a living, earned their daily oats, and made a contribution to the good of mankind.

Backyard horse practice sorta ranked with spayin' cats and trimming Chihuahuas' toenails.

That same kind of snobbery still exits, I think. Somehow, working on a valuable race horse, a Tennessee Walker show horse, an endurance Arabian, a Budweiser Clydesdale, Fred Whitfield's ropin' horse, Kristie Peterson's barrel horse, a New York City policeman's horse, a ranch horse, a rodeo bucker, a Quarter Horse cutter, an outfitter's pack mule, or a Lipizzan performer is interpreted as doing something more worthwhile than floating teeth on a backyard plug.

Those working horses have a purpose. That dignified your veterinary efforts, lends some value to your education and experience. All your acquired ability isn't being wasted in frivolous endeavor on a horse who isn't really "workin' for a livin'."

But, with all that being said, what's work to a horse? Is it something they feel good about? Does it give them a sense of self-worth? Of course not.

"Well, my little mare, I better finish this hay. Crooked Jack will be comin' to take me to the mall where I can walk in circles all day giving joy to little boys and girls."

"I'm so proud of you, Geldy. You bring so much happiness into the world."

Coyote Cowboy Proverb: Work to a horse is anything he does because you make him do it.

I tell people my horse likes to rope. Meaning, I guess, that he likes to chase cattle. But he spends a lot of time in the pasture with cows and calves. I've never seen him chase them on his day off.

Ah, but you good horsemen say, "This horse loves to run," or "He was born to buck," or "I can tell he loves to pull this plow. He can't wait for me to crack the whip!"

I see them run and kick up their heels in an open pasture . . . but not for long. Are they having fun? Can horses have fun? Are they bored? Can they get bored?

I'd be hard put to argue that they can't have fun, get bored, or get mad.

But horses are domesticated animals. Under the care and at the pleasure of those who pay for their keep. It is not their choice. It is ours. Like teenagers, if we give them room and board, we expect something in return. At our pleasure, even if our pleasure is team roping, showing Arabians, or just as a pet.

But in the end, it's all work to a horse. 🐴

Illustration by Don Gill

On the Edge of Common Sense

By Baxter Black

Horse people

Illustration by
Boots Reynolds

I WOULD like to talk to you about a certain kind of person who ranks in my mind with duck hunters. Now, don't get your gander up, I'm not gonna say anything about duck hunters. After all, what can you say about someone who gets up in the middle of the night, in the middle of the winter, then goes out and stands in water all day, up to his buckle, and then … shoots a duck.

But I'm not talkin' about duck hunters, no … the kinda people I'm talkin' about are horse people.

Yes, you may have one in your family. You know it when you sit down at the table with a horse person because the first thing they start talkin' about is horses. On and on and on. And if there's two of 'em you might as well get up and leave 'cause you aren't gonna get a word in edgewise.

And cowboys are the worst. You can be drivin' down the road—three of you in the front seat of the pickup—and you'll pass by this big ol' meadow. In it there'll be 52

sorrel geldings, each with one stockin' leg and a snip right on the end of his nose. The guy sittin' in the middle will point and say, "See that one 17th from the left … I broke him in 1993." How do you argue with somebody like that?

Or you go out to somebody's place, and they say, "Doc, it's good to see ya! I just got a brand new horse! I know you'll wanna look at him." See, they think because you're a veterinarian, that you care. Which, of course, I do!

Well, I have a confession to make … I have come to realize over the years that I have been a horse person all along. I sat there observing, just like you reading this column, the obsession of horse people with their beast, saying, "Yes, I know people like that!" Never realizing that I, too, was afflicted.

It all came into focus one cruel winter evening—minus-15 degrees, 20-mph winds, and snowing hard. Our company had just arrived. I had recently acquired a spectacular King Ranch gelding. I mean the brand alone was worth a hundred bucks!

In my excitement, I offered, "Listen, I've got a really dandy new horse. He's as shiny as a new dually, smooth as silk pajamas on a snake, light as feathers on angel food cake, and will eat truffles outta your hand. How'd you like to slip out to the corral and have a look?"

Out of the corner of my eye I saw my wife display an arched eyebrow … a sign of warning. Not unlike the one you see on a teamster's face when he's about to take the bullwhip to a wayward oxen. You've often seen it in Hillary's eyes.

She calmly said, "Honey, it's 20 below outside. The drifts are six feet deep between here and the barn, not to mention the fact that your mother is 80 years old."

ON THE EDGE OF COMMON SENSE | BY BAXTER BLACK

A Good Horse

He spent his last year living a horse's dream, being loved by a little girl.

A $400 dental bill at age 25 extended his life. I've owned many horses; he's the only one I've ever buried on my place. His greatest trait was that he had try.

"He was hard and tough and wiry, just the sort that won't say die…" was how Banjo Paterson put it in "The Man From Snow River."

He made a good cowman out of my daughter, won her a buckle in team penning. He never placed in the halter class, always a little overweight, a might short. I took a lot of hoorahin' from the well-mounted boys at the roping arena.

"But still so slight and weedy, one would doubt his power to stay and the old man said, 'that horse will never do.'"
–ibid

But after runnin' 20 steers he was still bursting out of the box, givin' his all, while the other boys were changin' horses or skippin' turns. And solid? Let me tell ya, even with my horseshoeing skills he stayed sound. Every time I'd buy another horse, and, like I said, I bought many, he'd become my backup.

"He wasn't my best but he was my ace."
Larry McWhorter,
"Blackdraught."

He was 13 when we bought him. He'd done ranch work and become a Little Britches all-around. When he was 17, he took my son for his first ride at age 0.

"A kid's horse needs a cool head. And with wise ol' Skeeter between their knees they was safe as if in their own beds."
–Gary McMahan,
"Skeeter."

At age 22, he moved to the ranch with us and started checkin' cows in the brush and rocks. My nephews and nieces and tenderfoot friends were his students. Never a plug, boss at the bunk, a voracious eater, he finally wore down. Despite the dental work and soft feed, his muscles melted away. But his spirit remained. That's when we found him a little girl. She weighed less than a saddle and block of salt. He stumbled a little at the trot, but she looked like a rodeo queen on his back.

"…To see a fine lady upon a white horse…."
–Anonymous,
"Ride a Cockhorse."

Now he's gone. Died in the night. Just quit breathin'.

*"Amigo, my friend, so true to the end
Eras buen caballo, amigo, my friend."*
–Les Buffman and Mike Fleming,
"Amigo."

I said a few words over him.
Now I've got to go tell the kids. 🐴

On the Edge of Common Sense

By Baxter Black

Veterinary Diagnostic Voice Mail

Illustration by Boots Reynolds

HELLO. You have reached the automated voice mail of Triple A Aardvarks Are Us—All Creatures Great and Small Veterinary Clinic, Animal Health Supply, Grooming, Boarding and Training, and Counseling Center. If you have a credit card limit of no less than five thousand dollars please press one. If not, please hold.

1. Thank you. If your problem concerns a pet—including dogs, cats, small rodents, reptiles, cockatiels, highway accidents, and other creatures where cost is no object—please press one. If you have livestock whose value is dependent on a fickle, unpredictable, often cruel market BUT you have a good job in town, a wife with a job, federal disaster insurance, or land and farm equipment that can be used as collateral, please press two.

2. If you have a poultry problem, press one for the chicken soup buyer. If you are a pork producer, press two for counseling and hysteria prevention. If your problem concerns cattle, press three.

3. If the condition is serious enough (over $500), and you can bring the animal to the clinic, press one. If the condition is not life-threatening, or you do not have a stock trailer, press two.

4. If you have already been treating this animal yourself for weeks, press one. If the animal is ambulatory, press one. If the animal is recumbent, press two. If the animal is comatose, press three.

5. If the animal has been down for less than two days, press one. If the animal is still eating and drinking, press one. If the animal is not eating but still has a detectable pulse and respiration, press two.

6. We have now reached the critical stage in this automated voice mail Diagnostic Situation Prognosis Assessment Device. Your prognosis is: poor to partly cloudy. Estimated cost $112. Add $5 for weekend and after-hours. Satisfaction barometer: three.

If you would like to have the veterinarian make a house call, press one. If you want to kiss it off and bite the bullet, press two for Jonansen's Hide and Tallow. Have a nice day.

> **On the Edge of Common Sense**   BY BAXTER BLACK, DVM

Blazing Cecum

I WROTE A BOOK TITLED *Blazin' Bloats and Cows on Fire!* It referred to the flammability of rumen gasses and the spectacular, but rarely harmful, occasions when they are ignited.

I assumed that the predilection for ignition was confined to ruminants but, as is often the case, I was thinking too small. Dr. Charlie broadened my horizons.

He and his esteemed equine veterinary colleague, Marvelous Marv, were on a house call to examine a 4-year-old colt with colic. The horse was a fine-looking chestnut, but the facilities were not up to par. It was raining a steady drizzle, and the horse pen was abloom in late-spring Colorado mud.

Marvelous Marv was not necessarily fastidious, but he made a point to dress professionally. A Windsor-knotted tie, Pendleton-wool sport coat and checkered English hunting cap set him apart from Dr. Charlie, who wore more practical coverall garb. When they arrived together, most assumed Marvelous Marv was the man in charge and Dr. Charlie was his valet.

They soon determined from the history of the patient being fed a garbage can full of lawn clippings, and the swollen, tight, high-right flank, that a gaseous cecum was the problem.

The lady owner fretted. She led the horse from the muddy pen into a small, very old, wooden storage shed. The doctors proceeded with their examination and concluded that the cecum would have to be punctured to relieve the pressure.

The concerned owner held the halter while Dr. Charlie prepped the right paralumbar fossa. He was doing it mostly by feel since the light was very poor.

"Hold him tight," he instructed the owner.

He poised the three-inch, 12-gauge needle, just as Marvelous Marv flamed his cigarette lighter. Whether it was to lend assistance or to light his pipe is irrelevant; it coincided with the puncture and release of the cecal gas, causing a fireball that whooshed and brilliantly lit the shed long enough for the owner to scream and the horse to bolt through the door!

From his position cringing in the corner and now with no eyebrows, Dr. Charlie could see his colleague trying to beat out the wall of burning cobwebs, which reached to the rafters, with his natty checkered cap.

Marvelous explained later to the trampled owner that they should have warned her. The procedure, he told her, was routine, to ensure that no flammable gas was left in enclosed areas.

"Thank you so much," she said.

On the Edge of Common Sense

By Baxter Black

The Horse Show Conversation

"A fine lookin' horse you've got there (*if yer into modern art*)
I had a horse like that one time (*but he wasn't very smart*)

I'd guess that he's part Thoroughbred (*and part Catahoula hound*)
You get him in a claimin' race? (*or at least the lost and found*)

Oh, really, you've got the papers (*I'd use 'em to train the dog*)
And he's outta He's California! (*No wonder he smells like smog*)

He seems a little bit feisty (*to have one foot in the grave*)
Yup, I've used Ace myself sometimes (*when there's somethin' left to save*)

What kinda bit have you got there? (*it looks like a calving tool*)
Oh, you invented it yourself. (*Do them Vise Grips make him drool?*)

Yea, I'll bet it sure does stop him (*like runnin' into a train*)
You must of built that tie-down too. (*Never seen one made outta chain*)

And where did you get those leggin's?
(*from a circus refugee*)
Well, most people like'm longer.
(*At least down to the knee*)

Good luck. I reckon yer up soon.
(*I'd hate to be in that wreck*)
You've already finished your class?
(*And haven't broken yer neck*)

Two firsts and honorable mention!
(*Whoa up! I'm way off the trail!*)
A fine lookin' horse you've got there"
(*maybe that sucker's for sale . . .*)

Illustration by
Kevin Cordtz

> **On the Edge of Common Sense** BY **BAXTER BLACK, DVM**

Large Animal Vets & Bronc Riders

THE PROFESSIONAL RODEO COWBOYS ASSOCIATION is making an effort to encourage more young people to participate in the bareback, saddle bronc and bull riding events. Simultaneously, the American Veterinary Medical Association is making an effort to encourage more students to become livestock and equine veterinarians. Does that mean more young people are less interested in riding or doctoring untamed large herbivorous animals? Exactly!

In both cases, the primary reasons given by the "non-interested" are that the work is too hard and the pay is not enough. American and Canadian young people, as a rule, have become more worldly, resigned to life, and content with the path most frequently traveled, i.e., team roping and pet practices. So, we are going about it the wrong way if we think 21st century America will furnish enough youngsters to fill the needs of PRCA or AVMA.

I would bet that the average U.S. high school student spends more time playing virtual sports and games in front of a screen than participating in real physical games and sports. A generation ago, this wasn't the case. Coincidentally, back then there was no shortage of large-animal vets and bareback riders, either.

I'm thinking if you want bronc riders and large-animal practitioners, you need to look somewhere other than civilized America. Someplace like Iran, Tierra del Fuego, Mongolia or Louisiana. And there's hope on the horizon. Already, last year's National Finals Rodeo had more rough-stock riders from Louisiana than from Rhode Island, Quebec and Kentucky, combined!

We should concentrate on luring bull riders from grittier places. Major League Baseball has done a wonderful job seeking hungry talent from places like Puerto Rico and the Dominican Republic. South America has been a good source of herders for American sheep ranchers. It's an easy jump from sheepherder to bareback rider, then on to dairy veterinarian.

Where do we begin? The easiest place to start would be the Mexican border. Illegal immigrants come here to work. They want to. The work is not too hard for them. The pay is enough. And we need them. Instead of deporting the illegals we catch, we should give each one, man or woman, a chance to ride a bronc and castrate a bull calf. If they appear to have the aptitude, we send them to a bull riding school or enroll them in a pre-vet major at bilingual schools like UCLA, New Mexico State or the University of Florida. Twenty years down the road, the problem would be solved!

Author's note: It is amazing how I can see through complex problems so clearly. No wonder Condeleeza calls so often. Now, on to the next sticky wicket: Miracle Whip or Hellmann's Mayo as the National Condiment?

RODEODIO

I used to ride bulls, till my brains came in!

> 66 **... And a hard way
> NOT to make a living.** 99

Rodeo, my favorite sport unless you count cowboy poetry.

I rode and I roped. I won a little money, and though I'm not a PRCA Gold Card holder, I am a fan!

I overheard two ol' timers sitting in the row in front of me at the National Finals. In the arena below us a bareback rider had slid back off his hand, then flipped forward still clinging to the riggin'. A freeze frame would have shown him legs spread, feet in the air, right arm horizontal, outstretched in the traditional cartwheel position. Back on fast forward, the hapless rider went out over the bronc's head, hit feet first, then was run over by the thundering beast!

The first ol' timer said, "Man, that's a hard way to make a living."

"Yup," said the second one, "And a hard way NOT to make a living."

There are elements of a real cowboy's life that are represented in professional rodeo, but it is like comparing a local rancher catchin' one hock at his own branding vs. a world champion tie-down roper getting it done in less than five seconds. The big difference is that the rancher knows how the calf got there, who the mama is, knows where it's going, and will keep the cow and calf well fed, healthy, and safe from harm. Then, if all goes well, the rancher will break even.

But speaking for that rancher, we'd love to rope one in the arena in less than five seconds . . . just once, to know how it feels. And we admire those cowboys who can.

On the Edge of Common Sense

By Baxter Black

The All Ranch Rodeo

'Twas a matchup made in Elko for the cowboys in the know
Called the Rough and Ready Knock Down Finals All Ranch Rodeo.
Now the Texans entered up a team they thought could never lose
When they bet their reps against the Jordan Valley Buckaroos.

You could tell from where they hailed if you put 'em up for bids,
All the buckaroos wore fancy scarves and Amish lookin' lids
While the Texans wore their jackets for the brush down in the draws
And them twenty dollar roll-yer-own, cheap Guatemalan straws.

It was Blucher versus Leddy, it was leggin's versus chinks
It was rye versus tequila, it was leppies versus dinks,
It was sagebrush versus cactus, it was ear tick versus fly,
It was Poco Bueno versus sloggers raised on alkali.

Illustration by Boots Reynolds

The Texans took an early lead, at ropin' showed their stuff,
  But the buckin' horse fandango showed the buckaroos were tough.
They branded in a dead heat, but in deference to the crowd
  Each side was harshly penalized for cussin' so dang loud.

So the teams were standin' even when the final contest came,
  UNTAMED UNGULATE EXTRACTION, wild cow milkin', by name.
They loosed the beasts together, left their calves to bawl and mill
  And the two teams fell upon 'em like hyenas on a kill.

The buckaroo a-horseback threw his forty-foot right.
  He dallied just about the time the Texan's loop came tight.
Their trajectories collided in a bawlin', buckin' wreck,
  The ropes and cows got tangled and they wound up neck to neck.

In the meantime two big muggers plus two others brave and bold
  Attacked the knot of thrashing hide and tried to get ahold
Of somethin', hoof or horn or foot or spur or can of snoose.
  Then, by accident some dummy turned the bawlin' calves a-loose!

There was hair and teeth and eye balls in the picture now and then,
  There was moustached lips and swingin' bags, some thought they saw a hen
Flashin' briefly through the dust cloud. Wild images remain;
  A painting done in cow manure, a mating sandhill crane.

To describe the cataclysm would create an overload,
  But a photograph was taken, and this is what it showed;
At the summit pointed skyward were the Texas mugger's toes,
  One arm around a buckaroo, his fingers in his nose.

Who, in turn was mounted sideways splayed acrost a baldy black
  Who was layin' on a milker who was smashed flat on his back.
The braymer cow was balanced on her head amidst the jag,
  While a Texan fought her baby for possession of the bag.

From the cyclone flew the milkers, bottles high for all to see
  Like two winos at a party, where the wine and cheese was free.
The buckaroo's hind leg was draggin' like he'd lost the farm,
  But he kept his place by clingin' to the Texan's broken arm.

When they fell across the finish line and tumbled in the dirt
  The judge declared the buckaroo the winner by a squirt.
Since the race looked pert near even, the judge said with a shrug,
  "The winner is the cowboy with the most milk in his jug!"

"I object!" cried out the Texan, "Our ol' cow just had three tits!"
  "That's a handicap," the judge said, "I admit it's sure the pits,
But the buckaroo, I noticed, too, was short a couple bricks,
  If you added all his fingers, he could barely count to six!"

ON THE EDGE OF COMMON SENSE | BY BAXTER BLACK

Poor Man's Ranch Rodeo

Working ranch rodeos are enjoying resurgence around the country. They allow ranches to enter teams and compete against cowboys from other ranches. They're often well-organized and can be pretty fancy events.

This has caused a minor disgruntlement among ranchers who, though officially qualified for the Working Ranch Cowboy's Association based on cow numbers and full-time employment, don't have the finances to hire full-time help. Tracy explained, in their case the neighbors all try to schedule their work together and hope nobody gets busted up, too bad. She says the concept of a four-man team isn't usually in the cards. If she and her husband can even get the banker or the town derelict for half a day's work, they consider themselves in tall cotton.

Team penning consists of the two of them, halfway mounted, in a wire pen with 200 Brangus cows and their bawlin' calves. It involves lots of yelling and dust.

Nor, she said, does the team doctoring resemble the official ranch-rodeo event. If she's alone and finds a sick one in the pasture, she sorts off the a) loco'd, b) pink-eye'd, c) prolapsed, d) all of the above, heifer and prods or chases it a jillion miles to the pens. If she and her husband are together, he ropes the beast and she runs down the rope to stab the critter with a needle without getting clotheslined, head butted, kicked or stabbed herself!

The winter Olympics version involves roping afoot in slushy snow and cowboy water skiing. The WRCA branding is the closest to the real thing on her ranch, except if you rope more than two by the neck you spend the rest of the day on the ground mugging.

Wild cow milking is a favorite event of many ranch-rodeo fans. On Tracy's place they do most of their wild cow milking in the squeeze chute on a rank, bad-bagged, fightin' cow that was supposed to have been sold last fall except she came up bred and a couple of perfectly sound, good tempered ones didn't. The hardest part is getting the witch back in the chute 4 days in a row till the calf can suck.

She said she enjoys the saddle-bronc and the wild horse race events. But only to watch. They haven't started green colts on their ranch since they raised their insurance deductible to $45,000. The last ranch rodeo that she and her neighbors combined to enter featured a saddled steer riding. (*Author's note:* Not a contest that seems destined for perpetuity). A bunch of Corriente roping steers are turned out. The roper rides out a'horseback, ropes a steer, team members saddle it and ride across the finish line. (*Author's note:* I can understand the cowboy mentality that invented such a great event). In Tracy's team's case, when 200-pound Fred swung aboard the Corriente it sank to the ground and became as boneless as a sleeping hound dog.

I don't know if we'll ever see a professional rodeo association that truly represents the cow business as Tracy lives it. But it's possible. After all, this is how we got women's mud rassling, bowling for dollars and reality TV programs.

ILLUSTRATION BY KEVIN CORDTZ

ON THE EDGE OF COMMON SENSE | BY BAXTER BLACK

Jess' Early Rodeo Days

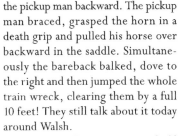

The National Finals Rodeo takes the spotlight every December in Las Vegas, Nev. The level of the competition and the animals seem to increase each year. It is easy to get swept up in the glitter and glamour of championship buckles and the full-volume extravaganza.

But the painful reminder of rodeo tradition comes back to the old riders every time a cowboy gets bucked off, a roper's loop snags the calf chute or a dogger gets rolled and flattened.

Jess said he was entered in a punkin-roller just south of Walsh, Colo., back in the old days. He'd stuck a good ride on a bareback bronc. He was using a brand new riggin' and was pretty proud. As his horse thundered down the arena fence, Jess plotted some way to make a spectacular dismount and land on his feet. The pickup man came ridin' hard between the galloping bareback and the fence. Jess leaned to the right and grabbed around the pickup man's neck. He then catapulted off his buckin' horse, over the pickup man's horse, thinking he'd drop lightly to his feet on the off side, tip his hat and wave to the crowd.

But all Jess's planning had not taken into account the proximity of the fence. He hooked a big spur into the netwire and locked up! He pulled

ILLUSTRATION BY RON BONGE

the pickup man backward. The pickup man braced, grasped the horn in a death grip and pulled his horse over backward in the saddle. Simultaneously the bareback balked, dove to the right and then jumped the whole train wreck, clearing them by a full 10 feet! They still talk about it today around Walsh.

Jess kept talking. One year he'd entered a mule rodeo in Boise City, Okla. Apparently they were more common in the 1950s. The wild bareback mule-riding event used bull ropes instead of riggin's. Jess was standing over his mule in the buckin' chute. His buddy Wimp helped him down. Jess dropped the tail end of his bull rope down the side of the mule.

Wimp waited for his signal to run the hook between the boards, underneath the girth and snag the bull rope. He tensed. Jess said, "Okay!" The day-dreaming gateman heard the cue, thought it was for him and swung the chute gate wide open. There was a moment within that fractured millisecond when Jess appeared to levitate above the mule, his legs spreading, his lips forming the shape of an O and holding a bull rope with nothing in it.

He actually did ride the mule the required 8 seconds, but managed to slap it multiple times with each and every free appendage including his chin and the soles of his feet, which disqualified him. Jess made a complaint to the stock contractor, casting blame on the inattentive gate opener. The stock contractor considered it, then refused his request for a reride. But he did offer him half the clown's pay. 🐎

On the Edge of Common Sense

By Baxter Black

The Ranch Horse Competition

Illustration by Ron Bonge

THERE'S A NEW competition being promoted by the Ranch Horse Association designed to show off the skills of cowboy and cow horse.

Pretty to watch. It includes among other things, reining, cutting and roping. When done properly it looks choreographed but since live steers and horses are involved you're never quite sure whose leading the dance. It is definitely a cowman's event, a minimum of chousing, charging or jerking the cattle.

I admit when I first heard of the event, a completely different picture came into my brain. One that would encompass all the situations a ranch horse might encounter in his daily chores.

I envisioned a race course that began on the top of a good-sized mountainside, like a ski slope. Matter of fact, the competition could be held at ski resorts during the summer, i.e. The Vail Stampede, Sun Valley Showdown or The Banff Blowout!

A yearling steer would be turned loose in the timber, given a thirty second head start, then the cowboy would break from the pines!

There would not be slalom flags on the hillside, but the finish line would be in a big meadow at the bottom of the hill in front of the ski lodge.

The hillside would be spotted with car bodies, boulders, abandoned Forest Service projects, bears, protesters, fire breaks, bobcats, elk antlers and pop-up hikers. A stock trailer would be parked in the meadow. The cowboy would have to rope the steer and load it to win.

Variations might be considered to make it competitive. Three untrained town dogs might be released from the trailer as they approach, or the cowboy could be required to cross a cattail bog in the meadow, or they could be chasing a prolapsed cow and have to replace it to win. Sounded good to me.

I could imagine the assembled crowds, lounging below, drinking cowboy drinks and wearing apré-cow wear. And it would be a timed event, of course, so it would have appeal to the ticket-buying spectators. Those same folks who enjoy professional wrestling, Bull-O-Rama or a public hanging.

Gosh, I like it already. 🐎

On the edge of common sense

By Baxter Black

Little Britches announcer

Illustration by Kevin Cordtz

I AM A keen observer of on-air radio and TV personalities, rambling professors, and occasional practicing politicians who are forced, on a regular basis, to fill dead air.

It is not an easy task for most people. Picture yourself introducing the guest speaker at the Pork Producers banquet when a note is passed up that the speaker had to have an emergency appendectomy. You are expected to entertain the assembled multitude until the emergency is handled, and you haven't prepared anything.

For most people, this would instill panic. But others I know would handle it with aplomb, and I admit I am one of the latter. In my case, I know where I developed that ability and honed my skill at filling dead air. I used to announce Little Britches rodeos.

"All right, ladies and gentlemen, our next contestant in the peewee flag race is little Bobby Roddy. Bobby is the son, third child, actually, of James and Sarah Roddy, who farm just south of Homedale. Go Bobby!

"Sarah, as most of you know …

"Kick 'im, Bobby … make him trot!

"Sarah operates an antique knick-knack shop on Highway 19 where you can buy baskets of dead flowers and wallpaper with ducks on it.

"Come on, Bobby, give him the over and under!

"Bobby is in the second grade at …

"Good, Bobby. Aim to the right; you're going to the wrong barrel. You need the one with the flag in it.

"Bobby's sister, Kerianne, was up earlier ridin' this same horse and she posted a blisterin' two-minute-59-second run, which leaves her in second place.

"Right, Bobby, grab the flag. Oh shoot … c'mon, you can ride back around. Now, grab it now!

"We should point out that Circle J Trailer was kind enough …

"Whoa, Bobby. Ya need to ride back and stick the flag in that can on the other barrel … no, the other, well, that's all right. Just put it wherever you want …

"Anyway, Circle J …

"Bobby! Bobby! This way!

"Lots of good sponsors help make this exciting event …

"Swing 'im back this way, Bobby! Ride toward that man with the red flag.

"We owe a great big thanks …

"Don, wake up! Whoa! Pull up, Bobby!

"Uh, we better get the paramedics out there to check Don. Anyway, how 'bout a great big hand for Bobby Roddy! His time is a sizzling three minutes 25 seconds!

"Our next contestant, Bobby's younger brother. …"

BAXTER
BLACK

ON THE EDGE OF COMMON SENSE

Illustration by Wally Badgett

THE VALDEZ

LATELY there has been some dissension at the rancho. I have overheard murmurings in the barnyard, in particular regarding my stock trailer. The grumbling animals enlisted my teenage daughter to present their complaints.

In my defense, let me describe my trailer. I felt like it was a real bargain when I bought it . . . let's see, in 1986. It's an 18-foot Hale, '71 model with a bumper hitch. On purchasing it from a reputable Hereford breeder, who guaranteed it would haul up to eight full-grown cows, I made a few minor repairs.

Three of the wheel bearings needed replaced, but the left front still spun good. We welded a jack on the tongue, built a new wooden panel for the endgate, put plywood over the rotting floor, and bought inner tubes for the two recaps that didn't have any tread left.

I'm still working on the wiring and have got a good coat of primer on the front panel, which covers about 6 square feet in the shape of the state of Utah. The greenish primer almost matches the original scour-yellow.

Recently I put down a rubber mat on the slick plywood after a horse came loose in transit and slid from front to back goin' up a steep grade. Every improvement an investment, I always say.

Jennifer's list of complaints seems trifling. The horses, she claims, are embarrassed to be seen unloading. She suggested I repaint it. Trying to get along, I pulled it down to the sand-blasting guy for an estimate. He recommended against it. Apparently he was afraid it would cause structural damage. To remove that much rust would weaken the steel.

Admittedly there has been some erosion where the sheet metal sides attach to the frame. This complaint was brought up by the cows. They worried about sliding a foot through the 4-inch gap that circles the trailer. I have always looked on that gap as good drainage to prevent manure buildup. I take it the boys at the sale barn agree, since they've named my trailer the Valdez (after the leaky oil tanker that made such a lasting impression in Alaska).

The dogs only asked that they be allowed to stay in the cab of the pickup instead of shut up in the trailer when I go into the sale. That way if they see any other dogs they can duck below the dash. I thought leavin' them in the trailer would keep other dogs from peein' on the tires. But they said no self-respecting dog would even consider it.

Perhaps my daughter has her own motives. I've noticed she won't even tie her horse to the trailer at a ropin' or horse show. I offered to paint her name on the side; give her some pride of ownership. She said no thanks. I've always admired her modesty.

Bein' a good ranch boss I'm considering their grievances, but I've good reason to avoid any hasty decisions. The Valdez is perfectly suited to my pickup. It's a '69 Ford with good tires and a fully functional left-side mirror. Besides, the annual registration fee for the trailer is only $13.

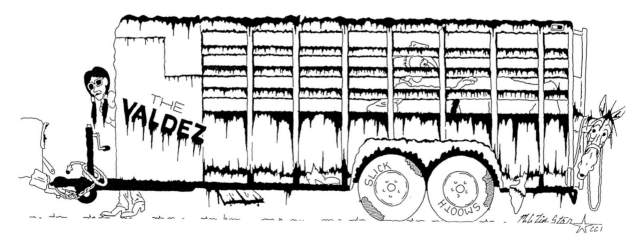

On the edge of common sense

By Baxter Black

Champion cowgirl

TED CALLED the other day to report that his 8-year-old daughter had announced she was going to become a barrel racer. Her first request was for a real horse trailer. The 16-foot stock trailer with the cow manure floor and faulty wiring would not suffice now that she'd made her career choice.

Ted related all this with the whipped-dog attitude of one who has just found out his new mother-in-law is a chronic sleepwalker and will be moving in with them for life.

I said, "Ted, didn't you go to the National Finals Rodeo?"

"Sure," he said, brightening. "Speed and Rich won the roping, Billy Etbauer smoked 'em in the saddle broncs, Fred won the all-around."

"Do you know who won the most money?" I asked.

"Well, Fred, I guess," said Ted.

"Nope, Sherry Cervi," I told him. "Matter of fact, she won $30,000 more than the next highest money-winner, man or woman."

I heard Ted drop the phone as the line went dead.

I understand. I remember when I saw the final tally for the 1999 Professional Rodeo Cowboys Association champions and discovered what Sherry Cervi had done. My first thought was the picture of the lady soccer player brazenly showing the world that women's athletics had scaled another mountain ... or two.

The soccer team's prowess and celebrity gave inspiration to womankind. Granted, many women athletes in recent history have distinguished themselves, particularly in golf, tennis, and the Olympic events.

Rodeo, too, has had its share of impressive women participants. But, like all other athletic events, it has been conceded that regardless of the women's ability, when competing head to head with men, they would lose.

Sherry Cervi changed that last December. Playin' by the rules, all set by men, she finished the season with the biggest paycheck in the PRCA. And if the association allowed women to enter the team roping, she'd probably have won enough in that event to leave Las Vegas wearin' the all-around cowboy buckle.

How 'bout that, Ted. Maybe you better start lookin' for a new trailer.

Sherry Cervi.

BAXTER BLACK

ON THE EDGE OF COMMON SENSE

Two Jumps

Illustration by Kevin Cordtz

Two Jumps said he used to ride bulls,
   in spite of his name, he tried;
he had grit, determination,
   and bravado on his side.

Unfortunately, he lacked skill;
   he was naturally inept,
and as life laid down her cowpies,
   that's precisely where he stepped.

But even a hard luck cowboy's
   entitled to one guru,
whose faith in him is undaunted,
   whose loyalty stays true blue.

Now all of the young bronc stompers
   and bull riders knew Lecille,
a rodeo clown and hero
   to all who strapped on the steel.

Lecille knew the bulls and broncs
   and always offered advice
on rodeo, on love, on life,
   on learnin' to sacrifice.

It was over the chutes at Knoxville
   when Two Jumps heard the phrase
that would stay with him forever,
   long after those heady days.

Lecille was walkin' toward him,
   no doubt, to wish him well.
Two Jumps cut eyes at his partners,
   to make sure they all could tell.

It was HIM Lecille had chosen
   to pass along for this ride,
the words he was meant to live by—
   he fairly bursted with pride.

Two Jumps was pullin' his bull rope,
   the rosin startin' to smoke,
when Lecille looked over the chute gate,
   squinted his eyes and then he spoke.

"Two Jumps," Lecille confided,
   "to really make yourself proud,
ain't no way you can ride this bull . . .
   so hang up and thrill the crowd!"

BAXTER BLACK

ON THE EDGE OF COMMON SENSE

DIED AND COME BACK TO LIFE

Have you heard of those folks who claim to have died
and then come back to life?
They speak of a glimpse of a heavenly place
far from the world and its strife.

The stories they tell have a common thread,
to a man they all contend
They found themselves in a long dark tunnel
with a light at the other end.

There are skeptics who doubt their descriptions;
they think it's mostly hot air.
But I can confirm they're not blowin' smoke,
'cause friends, I know, I was there.

I was entered up in the fall rodeo
and drawed a bull named Big Red.
Just when I had him, he bucked me clean off!
I lit right square on my head.

I hit the ground like a bag of loose salt,
knocked me plumb out, so they said.
Little stars twinkled around in my brain,
for all I knew I was dead.

I righted myself, or thought that I did,
I think I swallered my chaw.
But there I was in that long dark tunnel,
I shivered at what I saw.

'Cause down at the end just like they had said
a light materialized.
I squinted my eyeballs and studied that light,
it was then I realized—

I was peekin' out through a button hole;
it's true, I have no defense.
So I quietly pulled my shirt back down,
and crawled back up on the fence.

Illustration by Don Gill

ON THE EDGE OF COMMON SENSE | BY BAXTER BLACK

Bucking Horse Sale

I went to the Miles City annual Buckin' Horse Sale. I hadn't seen Montana so green since Noah ran aground!

It takes one back to when the West wasn't civilized. Today, in a time when athletes and audiences are coddled, one is reminded that many modern sports have evolved from more primitive survival skills, i.e. rock throwing to baseball, sword fighting to pool, spear to javelin, cannibalism to chili cook-off, alligator wrestling to bulldogging.

More than 200 broncs and bulls were bucked out during two days. After each ride, rodeo stock contractors bid on the stock. The riders were young men who were competing for a purse.

Many of us have adjusted to the glamorization of rodeo. Clothing and gear furnished by sponsors. Shirts, chaps, jackets, horse trailers, pickups, boots, hats, vests displaying product logos and mimicking the outfits worn by NASCAR pilots. Television coverage, glossy magazines with ads glorifying the spirit! All for the good of rodeo.

As I look back on the few years that I rode bulls, time has made my memory fuzzy. I had come to envision myself as a dashing, mature, buckle-bunny magnet, sort of a witty Ty Murray or a tall Larry Mahan. As I watched the 50 or 60 bull- and bronc riders behind the chutes at Miles City, the truth came back. Most of these cowboys were 18- to 22-year-old testosterone machines, fueled by each other's machismo.

Few had ever qualified for a pro rodeo card, but they were champs in the making. A gumbo stew boiling, one bubbling to the top every minute to strap himself on a beast, look fear in the eye, and say, "Gimme your best shot."

After the first, then the second, then third rides, the glamour was replaced by grit.

Truth is, most of these riders had second-hand equipment, well-worn clothes and not much meat on their bones. Their boots duct-taped, jeans patched, vehicles borrowed. As the afternoon wore on, the muddy arena played havoc with any fashion statement they might have intended. Hats were crumpled, shirts torn and bodies pounded.

And then I realized they were me.

When I began, I had no chaps, no Crockett spurs, only one hat, baggy jeans and a borrowed bull rope. I could taste the mud and dust, smell the slick Brahma hair and feel the adrenalin.

Saturday night at the street dance on Main, interspersed among the 2,500 reeling spectators, I could spot the contestants. They'd cleaned up a little, but not much. You knew the slick cowboy with the clean black hat, starched jeans and shiny boots had spent the afternoon in the grandstands!

But our heroes, who had to be sore, were surrounded by admirers (many female reliving each ride and not looking beyond this night's party. And the longer the evening wore on, the more glamorous they became.

That would be the feeling that prevailed and carried them to the next rodeo. I could feel it with them. Made me proud to be a cowboy! 🐎

On the Edge of Common Sense

By Baxter Black

Team Ropin' Conversation

Illustration by Don Gill

"THERE'S ONLY one thing worse than eating next to a left-handed person, and that's heading for him. It's like trying to screw the male end of a garden hose into the matching threads on your stock tank drain," so spoke Bob to Allen, two fair-to-middlin' team ropers, both fives, in the prime of their addiction. The equivalent of two-pack-a-day ropers.

"Yeah, team ropin's gone to hell," answered Allen. "Used to be, one guy had an arena, and twelve guys came to his place to rope. You got in good practice, lots of pretty good ropers, it was a social occasion too.

"Nowadays, everybody's got an arena, and nobody comes. You have to rope with your wife, and she's learning to barrel race. Fair is fair, so now all my rope horses run barrels too. And of course, she isn't interested in learning to heel, so you have to."

"Right," said Bob, "Denny Gentry ruined everything.

USTRC has made team ropin' so popular every horseshoer, ex-vet, and dairyman thinks he's Alan Bach."

"I know," said Allen, "it's also attracted so many social ropers with money that I'm embarrassed to buy a new trailer. Used to be the best ropers pulled to ropin's in their 12-year-old stock trailers with recaps and rust holes for ventilation. There wasn't enough money in ropin' to cover the cost of gas.

"At ropin's today there's so many duallies and three-horse slants with dressing rooms, it looks like a Arab horse show. And the guy can't even throw a rope!"

"I know what you mean," said Bob. "I've got a motley handful that come to my arena. I get to head, but it's a rare occasion they ever catch. I'm always havin' to offer constructive criticism or advice. It's like a continuing team ropin' clinic for the ability-deprived. There's one left-handed guy goes through horses like an Amish trader. He still thinks it's the horse's fault!

"But I'm lucky I've still got a few traditional heelers that come by. You know, fresh divorced, ridin' a horse that's for sale, and pullin' a '72 Hale two-horse rig. A *real roper* that gets there after you've wrapped the horns and drinks your beer. But at least I feel like I'm practicin' ropin' and not just practicin' practicin'."

"Yeah, they're in demand," sighed Allen.

Bob continued, "I've even fenced off an area in the arena for kids ... swing set, ropin' dummy, park bench with some shade. Sort of day care when they have the kids on weekends."

"Day care ... I like that," mused Allen.

"Yup," said Bob, "if you're gonna have your own arena you gotta learn to compete."

On The Edge Of Common Sense

By Baxter Black, D.V.M.

Serious Ropin'

Illustration by Boots Reynolds

If yer a sorry roper, friend, let me commiserate
and pass along some wisdom that may help to set you straight.

The reason that yer just no good and why you've never won
is . . . you've got the false impression that ropin' should be fun.

Don't kid yourself. It's just like golf. We're talkin' sacrifice!
To rope and win consistently you have to pay the price.

Eliminate those little things that busy up yer life.
Those bothersome distractions like house payments and a wife.

Quit yer job! Forsake the kids! Sell everything you own
and buy a dually gooseneck so you'll never be alone.

Then enter every jackpot where the fools'll take yer check
and practice till yer ropin' dummy's got a crooked neck!

Survive on beer and road food. Never falter, never fail,
'cause fingers will grow back, ya know, just like a lizard's tail.

Keep ropin till yer spoken word degenerates to grunts,
or simply, "I'm a heela, but sometimes I wope the fwonts."

And maybe you might beat the odds, but be prepared because
each dally man will have to face the roper's mentalpause.

Eventually the time will come when nothin' reconciles.
You'll be burnt out from front to back with cavities and piles.

Yer rope won't reach out like it did, yer loop just won't quite fit.
You can't remember if yer can is filled with beer or spit!

There's only one place left to go, so muster yer resources—
change yer name and get a loan, start trainin' cuttin' horses!

"I'm a heela—but sometimes I wope the fwonts."

On the Edge of Common Sense

By Baxter Black

The team roper's credit card

Illustration by Don Gill

CARL TOLD me the other day that one of his team ropin' buddies boasted he'd gotten a platinum credit card! I was taken aback. It was like being told that a serial killer had been granted knighthood, or the starling had been named the state bird of Idaho.

My first thought was, "My gosh, he robbed a bank!"

"No," said Carl, "and he was a real team roper too. Not some land developer or football player who pulls a three-horse slant trailer with a dressing room and has a sky box at the National Finals Rodeo every year."

"Well," I said, "we can eliminate getting a job, and he couldn't get a loan. Maybe he found a lotto ticket."

"No," said Carl.

"Let's see. He might'uv found a sack of money

in a 7-11 restroom. Or sold a good horse."

"Could have," nodded Carl.

"Sold a good horse, you mean?" I asked.

"Oh, I thought you said stole a good horse. No, neither one."

"Maybe he endorsed something ... like duct tape, or Butazolidin, or old inner tubes. Or he could have patented a new way to hang the wiring so it looks like the trailer actually has lights."

"No," said Carl, "but good things to consider."

"How about, he sold his used horseshoe collection? Or spare tire? Hey, I know! He could have donated blood or working body parts in a living will, or signed up to take experimental pharmaceuticals in some kind of test."

"All great guesses," said Carl, "but no."

"Okay. It's a sure bet he didn't get it feeding cattle, investing in the stock market, or by scrimping and saving. He could have ... no, it's not possible."

"What?" asked Carl.

"It's a long shot, but he could have won a roping."

"Ha, ha, ha, ho, ho, guffaw, snort, snicker, sigh ... ."

"No," I said, "I guess not. Well, if he didn't rob a bank, how did he get it?"

"Easy," said Carl. "He married a banker." 🐎

ON THE EDGE OF COMMON SENSE | BY BAXTER BLACK

Meals on Wheels for Roping Steers

KEVIN CORDTZ

Jessie Winchester wrote a song called "Mississippi on My Mind." It contained the line, "Where the dogs are hungry all the time." The same can be said about team-roping steers. They're bred to stay thin and rarely are they overfed.

Shannon had a little arena and always kept a handful of *flaco corrientes* (svelte bovidae). He asked Byron to find him some cheap hay and offered to let him use his homemade, flatbed fenderless trailer. In a couple of days, Byron located a stack of Hi Gear that'd been baled during the previous administration and put up wet. Byron got it for a dollar a bale. He managed to get 60 bales on the old stout trailer and started for Shannon's.

Just a few miles down the road, Byron began to smell smoke. He scanned the passing farms. It wasn't the right time of year for Mesilla Valley farmers to be burning ditches. The answer appeared in his rearview mirror. The bales were stacked on top of the tandem-axle tires. Friction was busy igniting the hay!

Byron panicked and called Shannon on his cell phone. The answering machine picked up. It was a raspy but enthusiastic voice advising any interested caller that Shannon's Arena and Livestock Exchange had ropings three days a week, boarded horses, did excavation, hoof-trimming, horse chiropractory and drywall. Please call back or leave a message, adios y'all…beep.

"Shannon! It's Byron! The trailer's smoking! Call me!"

Cars were whizzing by, honking and pointing. Flickers of fire could be seen, fanned by the headwind.

Punch, punch, punch … seven times. "You have reached Shannon's Arena and Livestock Exchange. Team Roping every Tuesday, Wednesday … etc."

"Shannon! The hay's on fire! Call me!" Byron swerved his pyrotechnic hay wagon into a gravel clearing. He mashed on the brakes, and three flaming bales toppled off the right side in front of the Land of Enchantment Nursing Home.

Punch, punch…seven times. "You have reached…etc."

"Shannon! We're cooked! Call me!"

Well, between the nursing-home garden hose and the local fire department, Shannon's hay and trailer tires were soon soaked and out of danger. Byron proceeded on and parked the rig in Shannon's arena.

As everyone knows, it's impossible to extinguish a stack of burning hay. Two days later, it was warm to the touch. Every time a bale was pulled off it'd hit the oxygen and flame up. Shannon finally scattered the mess as best he could and turned 30 hungry roping steers onto it. They ate it with relish. Byron said it was no wonder: "It's not everyday they get a hot meal!" 🐎

BAXTER BLACK

ON THE EDGE OF COMMON SENSE

The Missing Link

Illustration by Wally Badgett

IT ARCED across the cloudless sky like someone throwin' chum,
but they weren't fishin', no my friends, the object was a thumb.
It launched from Kenneth's dally when his heelin' rope came tight
and whizzed by Eddie's horse's head and disappeared from sight.

Eddie did a double take . . . hors d'oeuvres flashed through his mind,
a little sausage on a stick that looked like Frankenstein.
"Are you okay?" he asked when Kenneth finally took a breath.
His ropin' glove was crimson red, his face was white as death.

"Yeah, help me find my thumb," he said. "I better go, I think."
"You go," said Ed, "I'll bring it when we've found the missing link."
The next day Eddie got a call from Kenneth's lawyer friend.
"A suit," he said, "for negligence, is what I recommend."

Well, Eddie was surprised a bit, "We packed his thumb in ice.
We emptied out the beer and pop, a real sacrifice.
And put it in the cooler, then we rushed it straight on down.
I even got a ticket speedin' comin' into town.

"I've had some past experience. It's happened here before."
"Well, we'll concede," the lawyer said, "your service was top drawer.
The packing job was excellent, but in the final sum,
In spite of all you did for Ken, you brung us the wrong thumb."

ON THE EDGE OF COMMON SENSE | BY BAXTER BLACK

Brush-Popping "Fighter Pilot"

It's as close to being a fighter pilot as I'll ever come. As a college youth plotting my future, I had, on two different occasions, taken the physical and written exams to apply for Officer's Candidate School to become a Navy pilot. Fate intervened and those dreams went the way of "song-writer" and "car designer." I stayed the cowboy I always was. Never a regret.

Cowboys who ride where the mesquite and catclaw are thick are called brush-poppers. It's grand to be in the company of good, fearless cowboys who trust their horses. When a beast breaks out of the bunch you're bringin' in on a gather, the race is on! Range cows, as I've pointed out to the unfamiliar, are often as close to wild animals as one can come without requiring a hunting license. They're like discount-store employees; you can't actually walk up to one. They're domesticated, not tame. They're fleet of foot, frighteningly fast and will quit the bunch and never look back. If they break out on your side, you better have your cinch tight 'cause you're in for a ride.

A 300-pound, part-bramer baldface calf can run like a deer. It's out of sight before you get your horse swung around. Trying to outrun one to turn it back will test a horse. In the space of 5 seconds, you're at a dead run. The ground is rocky; the arroyos come up like bad guys in a video game, some so quick only your horse sees them. Same for the dreaded barrel cactus or horse-crippler.

As the screen in front of you is flashing by, you're watching for small spaces

between the brush or the occasional clear ridge for a glimpse of the calf. You're also clicking your eyes forward, sighting down the barrel of your horse's head between his laid-back ears, all at a pace as fast as you can urge your horse to run.

Hat pulled down, feet heavy in the stirrups, sittin' light, horse and reins in one hand, rope in the other, spurs dug in. A cow on a cow trail can go under a limb 16 hands high. So can a horse. The only thing stickin' out is you. Duckin' and divin' after a bunch-quitter is like sitting in the front seat of a roller coaster. The horizon and air speed indicator constantly tilt and whirl. You balance like a gyroscope over your horse. You're

hunting a hole or a crack in a solid wall of 12-foot-high mesquite, catclaw, agave, cholla and whitethorn that slap and scrape your leggings and tapaderas, that rip and scratch your shirtsleeves, hands, and ears, that jerk at your rope, punch your ribs and float your stomach. Split-second decisions, always hoping that the limb will break, the calf will turn or the throw is good.

Speed and uncertainty; exhilarating. Trusting a big-hearted horse; power. Catchin' the runaway at the end of a long rope; all in a day's work. Brush-popper. 🐎

ON THE EDGE OF COMMON SENSE | BY BAXTER BLACK

Hey, Cowgirl, Need a Ride?

You can talk about the glamour
   and the love of rodeo
The challenge and the heartbreak
   of the dally and the throw
Of the guts and of the glory,
   the leather and the sweat
The gristle and the power
   of the bull that ain't rode yet

And the get up-in-the-morning
   and the miles-down-the-road
And the bronc that stands awaitin'
   and the rope that ain't been throwed
The vision of the buckle
   worn by superhuman champs
And paid for in contusions,
   broken bones, in aches and cramps

And mothers in the bleachers
   and spouses back at home
Who keep the home fires burnin'
   while their darlin' loved ones roam
The siren's call of rodeo
   that beckons one last ride
The gambler's itch, the mountaintop,
   the pinnacle, the pride

The reason they give all they have
   is measured in a score
A crowd, a millisecond,
   flag and timer, judge and roar
But for some the lure is simpler,
   the attraction that still pulls
Like me … just gettin' girls
   was the reason I rode bulls!

COWBOY PHILOSOPHY

It's like being trapped between two horse people in a pickup on Highway 75 from Coffeyville to Okmulgee; you'll never get a word in edgewise!

> **"** It's the truth in humor that makes it funny! That's why there are no science fiction jokes! **"**

Most of my poems and stories come from events that folks tell me or send me. I am often heard to say, "I can't make up stuff that is crazier, more bizarre, or more unbelievable than what really happens!" It's the truth in humor that makes it funny! That's why there are no science fiction jokes.

This section is apart from the action stories so common in my column. This section includes my observations of us, our way of life, the animals in our care, the cowboy mentality, the holes in the queen's underwear, our left-handed logic and the occasional attempt to explain why we are the way we are.

Through it all, I hope, comes a sense of what we value: friends, the animals, people who try and make the best of things, our lifestyle and God's place in our lives.

We recognize the small but important part we play in the environment, our community, our church, charitable organizations and making others' lives better.

I'm reluctant to title this section *Cowboy Wisdom*. After all, Solomon or Lincoln or Supreme Court Judge Sandra Day O'Conner would never have included a piece called, *The Cowboy's Document of Contrition*. Of course, Lincoln probably never owned a weed-eater.

97

ON THE EDGE OF COMMON SENSE | BY BAXTER BLACK

Why America Needs Cowboys

1. **So the press will know how** to describe people who don't mind taking the handoff and running over the middle on a fourth down and two-foot situation.

2. To prevent the abuse of facilities, i.e. corrals, calf chutes, barbed wire, aluminum gates, telephone poles, old car bodies, split rails or electric fence. When properly placed, the cowboy can be sandwiched between these inanimate objects and the cow, to soften the blow and lessen the damage.

3. To serve as one of the few sources of amusement in a cow's life.

4. To serve as an example of a job description that's routinely excluded from such actuary lists as "most dangerous," "lowest paid," "longest hours" and "life expectancy," because cowboys can't afford insurance anyway. I mean, who'd insure a bootjack, a plastic whip or a rubber hubcap hammer?

5. To stand as a reminder of what you can become if you don't do well in math, English or study hall.

6. There will always be a need for laboratory rats in experiments examining the chaos theory, Murphy's Law and what's loosely called "Job's affliction."

7. To act as a buckle-bunny magnet.

8. To serve as inspiration for the Charlie Russell, Roy Rogers and Louis L'Amour wannabes.

9. To prove that no matter how good you are at somethin', you can always get bucked off!

10. To show that being a male chauvinist pig doesn't pay...well.

11. To shine as an icon of truth, justice and the cowboy way.

12. To lend credence to the belief that underneath that stoic, romantic image painted on the silver screen is a simple human being with feet of cow manure.

13. And finally, the world needs cowboys for the same reason we need knights, punt-returners, banjo players and Marines. You have to have someone you can send in first. 🐎

On The Edge Of Common Sense

By Baxter Black, D.V.M.

ANIMAL LOVERS

Let's talk about animal lovers,
　not those who protest and accuse,
But everyday people who carry the load
　and don't make the 6 o'clock news.

It's proper to make the distinction
　when explanations are given,
Between those who care as a hobby
　and others who care for a livin'.

When we speak of animal lovers,
　the part-time groups come to mind—
Nice-enough folks, who articulate well
　and shine when the cameras grind.

It's too bad more credit's not given
　to the ones who seldom get heard.
'Cause, in spite of their modest behavior,
　their actions speak louder than words.

These are the folks, that on Christmas Day,
　take care of God's animals first.
With never a thought they should have the day off,
　or that they might be reimbursed.

They believe that Genesis meant it,
　that man has dominion o'er all.
And they don't take their mandate too lightly,
　to care for the great and the small.

God's entrusted His creatures to us
　by rating us all in a log,
According to what our abilities are;
　most get a house cat or dog.

But the bulk of the animal kingdom
　He placed in the hands of a few
Who feel more at home in a pasture than
　an office on Fifth Avenue.

God did it that way for a reason,
　'cause talk's cheap where carin's concerned.
The title of animal lover is
　an honor that has to be earned.

To those who'd debate my conclusion,
　to your own you're welcome to cling.
But I'll bet if we'd ask His opinion,
　God knows that He did the right thing. 🐎

OIL PAINTING BY STEVE DEVENYNS

❯ On the Edge of Common Sense

BY **BAXTER BLACK, DVM**

Anthropomorphism

ANTHROPOMORPHISM IS A WORD that has often been used in a negative context by people in the livestock business. By definition, it is the ascription of human characteristics to things not human—particularly animals.

In our continuing effort to raise animals for meat purposes humanely, we confront huge moral, biological, spiritual and logical differences that distinguish man from beast. Yet, we who spend our lives caring for animals know better than most that incidents occur that cannot be explained or denied.

Horse people know that bonds exist between horses. "Buddy" relationships are established if horses are penned closely for a period of time. Take out just one of them for a ride and the other will nicker and pace, and watch every new arrival until his buddy is back. At which time they may renew their biting, bullying and trash-talking with each other!

"Just like my brothers and me," I remark, anthropomorphizing.

Gary's 31-year-old mare died of old age. Her 20-year-old gelded offspring and two other horses were in the pasture with her. On the advice of his veterinarian, Gary left the dead body unburied for three days. Allow the other horses to grieve, the vet had said.

Gary said the offspring stood vigil over the mare's corpse. After she was buried, he saw the gelding pawing the grave, eventually scooping out a good-sized hole before he gave up. Was he trying to bring her back?

When my old dog, Hattie, didn't come into the backyard for the night, I went ahead and locked up her co-dog, Pancho. Next morning, Pancho and I went out to feed. I called for Hattie. Finally, I asked Pancho, "Where's Hattie?" He took me west, out of the corrals, up into the horse pasture, all the way to the far gate. There she was. She had died in the night.

I buried her immediately. Pancho went off feed. Every morning for several days, when I let him out of the yard, he would go straight to her grave and lie beside it. Try as I might, I cannot explain what I think was going on in his mind without using terms that describe human emotions.

Maybe that's the way it should be. We aren't supposed to know everything. 🐎

On The Edge Of Common Sense

By Baxter Black, D.V.M.

Political Correctness

Illustration by Robert M. Miller, D.V.M.

*I*T'S COMING! Political correctness in the animal kingdom! I have conferred with those fervent homogenizers of the once-colorful and descriptive English language to formulate the following list:

STRAY DOG.

Both words are unacceptable. They imply that a four-legged mongrel is subsisting as a vagrant. We have chosen the term *misdirected wagamorph.*

MUSTANG.

Definitely out. Associated too much with an automotive corporation. We are going to protect them into extinction. They shall henceforth be called *adoptable equine derivatives.*

KILLER WHALE.

Need I say more? The name suggests that these beautiful creatures would rather kill and eat living things than down a kelpburger in the shape of a baby seal. We're calling them the *masked cetacea.*

FAT STEERS.

Entirely out. No slur shall be made about their weight or their sexual predicament. Each cattle buyer will now deal in *ready edibles.* No, that won't work either. How 'bout *Ripened Ruminants?*

GOMER BULL.

Of course, any allusion to sex must be eliminated. The term "gomer" really has no meaning, but leaves one with the impression that he's one brick shy of a load. And though he's certainly one something shy of a load, the association with *Mayberry RFD*

A partially horn-impaired Special Himherford Dire. (A Dire can serve as either a Dam or Sire. It is regionally called a Sam.)

must be downplayed.

He shall hereinafter be christened a *misguided chromosome depositor.*

QUARTER HORSE.

No chance. The hypersensitive could interpret that to mean he's three-quarter something else. I've coined the term *dollar horse.*

POLLED HEREFORD.

Come on, now! Wouldn't it be less discriminatory to rename them the *unhorned himherford?*

Too many of our creatures were named by that original chauvinist, Adam, with unconscious patronizing references to sex, gender, race, religion, size, handicap, mental state, congenital deformity, or odd behavior.

Consider how insensitive we are to call something a nanny goat, a laying hen, praying mantis, peafowl, woodpecker, short-nosed sucker, or a turkey.

I admit I've been called a turkey, but I thought it was a step up from the dodo.

But if we are truly worried about the political correctness fad, what are we gonna call a cowboy? A *two-legged ungulate overperson?* Why not?

"Git along little disenfranchised mobile nurture seeker."

ON THE EDGE OF COMMON SENSE | BY BAXTER BLACK

The Vanishing Cowboy — Myth or Reality

ILLUSTRATION BY RON BONGE

Let us explore the vanishing cowboy — myth or reality. First *let's* consider a truly vanished icon, the mastodon hunter.

All that remains of this mighty figure are a few paintings on a cave wall. That, and a book cover or two with him in a furry loincloth posing with his spear and a Raquel Welch look-alike complete with bear-skin bikini and shaved legs.

Why did this once powerful caveman vanish? Because the prehistoric Fish & Game outlawed hunting mastodons? Because they became vegetarians? No ... it was because they ran out of mastodons.

The legacy of the proud mastodon hunter is now kept alive by Cabelas, L.L. Bean, Remington, "The Flintstones," Tarzan, Charlton Heston, the Olympics and the Discovery Channel.

Back to the vanishing cowboy. There are many categories of cowboys, i.e., cowboy artists, rodeo cowboys, trail-riding cowboys, cowboy poets, cowboy singers, line-dancing cowboys, movie cowboys and others who exist to glorify or imitate the real thing.

But unlike the mastodon, we haven't run out of cows. Many will be quick to point out, especially when the market is low, that we have too many. It's also true that in some parts of the world cows are commonly raised without cowboys; New Dehli, Kenya and Indianapolis, to name three.

On earth there are vast expanses of grazing land that aren't suitable to farming, like Queensland, Mongolia, the Russian Steppes, the Argentine pampas and Wyoming. These are places where four wheelers dare not go: deep canyons, mesquite thickets, mountain tops, slippery slopes and river crossings.

Those machinery-unfriendly spots are suitable to cows and best tended by men a'horseback. To ride the rim, to check or gather, to pop 'em outta the brush, to ford the mountain stream and push 'em out the other side is most easily accomplished if one can follow in the cows' footsteps.

I feel like this is true even in places like the Ozarks of Missouri or the hollers of West Virginia.

So, if the cowboy is to vanish, we must first dispose of the cows in these otherwise unreachable locales. We must eradicate or outlaw cows in most of Australia, most of western Canada and the United States, and the heart of Argentina, just as a start.

Which would create the inevitable Catch 22: By reducing the number of indigenous cows to the point of extinction, we would automatically kick in the endangered-species act.

To protect them, the government would have to hire men a'horseback to manage the declining herds. It becomes a never-ending, self-perpetuating circle. Cows and cowboys.

In conclusion, the vanishing cowboy some talk about wistfully, is a myth. But how would they know if he was vanishing if they never left the freeway? I can assure you he's still out there chasin' them new mastodon. You just can't see him from the road. 🐴

ON THE EDGE OF COMMON SENSE | BY BAXTER BLACK

Wisdom of the Ages

Grandpa has a special job, and has since days of yore,
To teach his children's children things his parents might ignore.
Like how to spit and whistle, carve initials on a tree,
The value of an empty can and why some things aren't free.

Why dogs get stuck, how birds can fly, why grandma's
  always right
And how to tie a square knot and the time to stand
  and fight.
And, if Grandpa's a cowboy, and the kid is so
  inclined,
The horn of wisdom empties out to fill his little mind.

He has the kid upon a horse as soon as mom allows
And fills him full of stories 'bout the old days punchin' cows,
And how when he was "just your age" he rode the rough-
  string snides
And never hesitated, see, that's how he learned to ride.

So when the horse the kid was ridin' tossed him to the ground,
The grandpa said, "Now get back on, don't let him keep
  you down."
The boy balked, but grandpa knew the lesson to
  be learned:
"One of us must ride this horse," he said, his voice stern.

Then wisdom passed from old to young. "Yer right," the
  kid said true,
"You want I let the stirrups out…just one hole or two?"

ILLUSTRATION BY KEVIN CORDTZ

On the Edge of Common Sense

By Baxter Black

Life Is a Compromise

THEY TELL me Walter is smokin' again,
  But life is a compromise.
He's tried to kill himself so many ways,
  The heart was not a surprise.

I guess he's lucky they found him in time—
  Was close, I understand.
Pickups on dirt roads at breakneck speeds,
  Would'a killed a lesser man.

The nurses said he was pleasant at times . . .
  When he was anesthetized.
But alas, he relapsed back to normal,
  His arteries revulcanized.

It was awful to watch his recovery,
  His forced marches down by the wood.
Striding along in his tennies and
  He's quit eating everything good.

Begrudgingly he's getting better,
  Got horseback, but some things have changed.
He's growin' a beard and he's writing
  His memoirs out on the range.

He's givin' the kids a little more slack,
  At runnin' the home ranch outfit.
Of course, they threatened to leave him next time,
  If he didn't back off a bit.

So he's still the biggest buck in the herd
  And goes around leavin' his scrape,
And buglin' some . . . but he's careful now
  'Bout who he gets bent outta shape.

So, the fact I hear that he's smokin' again
  Is sort of what I would expect.
With his rebuilt heart he's prob'ly deduced
  There's nothin' left to protect.

I asked if his doctors agreed with his scheme,
  He said, "Nope, their warnings were stern,
Said sooner or later they'd see me again . . .
  But they wouldn't be near as concerned."

Illustration by
Dwayne Brech

On the Edge of Common Sense

By Baxter Black

Everybody's good at something

Illustration by R.M. Miller, D.V.M., Ph.D.

NOBODY ENJOYS watching a good horseshoer more than an "average" horseshoer. I noticed it one afternoon when Big Red was shoein' my horse. I normally shoe my own horses, but he offered to give me some pointers. Luke watched as intently as I. The rest of the cowboys didn't pay as much attention. Either they were experts or didn't shoe their own horses. But Luke and I didn't miss a nip or a clinch.

Maybe that explains televised golf. To the ungolfer like me its popularity is unfathomable. It would be like televising a haircut from a Cessna at 1,200 feet.

"He's addressing the ball, Morton, a good 2 iron or 4 wood from the

The new glue-on shoes worked for some farriers, but Harry was simply too slow, and the glue dried too fast.

pin, which lays beyond that dogleg to the right. He's got a bad lie there between that concrete bridge abutment and that 100-pound trash bag full of styrofoam pingpong balls. Not able to get a full backswing, he has grasped his club like an ax … the swing! My gosh, Morton, he's chipped the cinder block, burst the bag, and the air is filled with a blizzard of white balls … he's still flailing! Look out, Mor …!" Whack!

I can understand the fascination of an amateur, or budding, or simply poor golfer. They are hoping to glean some tidbit from a master that will improve their own game.

I enjoy music and play the guitar. It is always a pleasure to watch a good guitar player. Fingers contorted into graceful shapes, dancing on strings, crawling up the neck like a spider. I will back up a cassette over and over to hear the same guitar lick that thrills me. My interest is kindled by the misguided hope that if I practiced long enough, I could make that sound.

My interest in, and effort at, team roping falls in the same category. I enjoy it so much it's almost not fun. But I am ready to concede that regardless of my passion or obsession, it takes more than dedication to achieve mastery. It takes natural talent.

The talented don't have to work as hard at something to be good at it. But if they do, they are unbeatable: Ty Murray, Tiger Woods, Reba McEntire, Michael Jordan. Big Red, the horseshoer, is like that. No matter how hard I studied and worried and tried, I would never possess the "feel" or the "instinctual knowledge" he has that surpasses even experience.

Which leaves me some consolation and the Coyote Company proverb that says, "Everybody's good at something."

On the Edge of Common Sense

By Baxter Black

Johnny Was a Mule Man

JOHNNY WAS a mule man, which says a lot to me.
  His motto: Keep it simple. Lay it out for me to see.
If a kid can't understand it, it's pro'bly bound to fail.
  He'd rather have a good man's word than a contract in the mail.

He never trusted horses or computers on the shelf.
  He'd rather count the cattle, check the pasture for himself.
If he knew you knew your business, he'd back you to the hilt,
  And gladly give the credit for the fences that you built.

But he'd ride you like a blanket so you couldn't go astray
  'Cause to him it all was pers'nal . . . he knew no other way.
He didn't have the answer to each problem you were heir.
  But he figgered you could solve'm. That's why he put you there.

If you could tie a diamond hitch or pour the ol' concrete
  That meant as much to him as runnin' out a balance sheet.
See, he knew that all the business in the end came down, somehow
  To a single salaried cowboy who went out and checked a cow.

I guess he always thought himself not one of the elite.
  But a man who works for wages and just got a better seat.
And I'm sure he spent some sleepless nights doubting what he'd done,
  But he trusted his opinion more than almost anyone's.

So, if he prayed, which most men do, when sleep is closing in,
  He pro'bly prayed that Scottish prayer that suited men like him,
"Lord, grant that I am right, that my judgment's not gone blind,
  For Thou knowest in Thy wisdom, it's hard to change my mind."

Illustration by Mike Craig

> ## On the Edge of Common Sense

BY **BAXTER BLACK, D.V.M**

Johnny the Mule Man Revisited

ILLUSTRATIONS BY KEVIN CORDTZ

JOHNNY WAS A MULE MAN. That's a statement of fact and also the name of a poem I once wrote.

To me, there are two sides to mule people, the brainy side and the stubborn side.

They're deep thinkers mostly because they always feel the need to explain why they ride mules. This creates a natural stubbornness because mules are smarter than horses, and mule people are indignant that everyone doesn't know that!

Johnny liked mules because he wasn't comfortable with horses. He liked to look at them, but I think they were too frivolous, too "fragile" for him. He didn't have time for nuance   with animals or employees. I suspect, though he's long dead, he'd lump the modern gentle horse-training techniques in with "time outs" for undisciplined children and investing in miniature cattle.

"It's great to become one with your horse, but do it on your own time!"

He liked to buy mules for the sheep camp. They weren't always well-broke, but that didn't faze him. He counted on the Basque sheepherders to be tougher than the mules. Not more clever, or stronger, or even smarter, just tougher. He was Basque himself and knew how tough they were. Mentally tough, confident, stubborn, belligerent, hardheaded, mulish you get the idea.

But he also had a genius for seeing through the smoke and obstacles of a problem. One year, we needed a large number of cows for newly acquired ranches. In spring, the feedlots were full of cattle. He told me to breed all the light feeder heifers in the feedlot. He didn't tell me how, he just said, "Do it!"

I did. Sixty rented Angus bulls, plus 30 days, plus 1,250 heifers, plus a 62 percent conception rate equals the longest six weeks I ever spent calving heifers!

Johnny didn't visualize the process, but he could see the goal. He left the "how to" and the "details" up to those of us who worked for him. It was an excellent training ground for someone who'd someday be trying to make a living as a cowboy poet. Particularly since it's illegal to publish poetry in the United States.

The life lessons I learned from Johnny the Mule Man were: 1. How to win the game when you don't know the rules. 2. How to find your way when you don't have a map. And, 3. When someone tells you it can't be done, what they mean is they can't do it.

On the Edge of Common Sense

By Baxter Black

Women and Mules

Illustration by Kevin Cordtz

He's got a black hat and he's broke
He's lean as a bicycle spoke
   The fire in his eyes
   It ain't no surprise
He's a cowboy, that ain't no joke

If yer lookin' fer help, he's fer hire
He'll spur that bronc down to the wire
   Or break him to ride
   And rope either side
But don't ask him to sing in the choir

He's no good with a wrench in his hand
At milkin' or plowin' up land
   But give him a rope
   A horse at a lope
His purpose you'll soon understand

He camps out some nights on the ground
He's no good at settlin' down
   If it don't seem fair
   He'll say he don't care
Say, Bossman, I'll see you around

And ladies, he's usually bad news
He's good for a case of the blues
   But with a guitar
   In a smokey ol' bar
He'll charm you right out of your shoes

To scope him you don't need a key
Just remember he'll always be free
   If that's good enough
   Then it shouldn't be tough
Ya pretty much git what ya see

He plays kinda loose with the rules
And hardput to tolerate fools
   But he's good with a horse
   And children, of course
But he's hell on women and mules

On the Edge of Common Sense

By Baxter Black

Carol's story

Illustration by J.P. Rankin

CAROL'S STORY is just another glamorous tale of a city girl who married a romantic Nebraska Sandhills rancher 17 years ago and became a "vocational cow assistant" for life.

"So what exactly do you want me to do?" she asked.

"Take the pickup (she didn't learn to drive till she was 29), then go out there to the Big Pasture (the dreaded Big Pasture, where one grass-covered hill looks like the next one to her). Start way back there at the gate in the Middle Pasture where we have the heifers now and honk. They'll come follow you, and we'll just run 'em up through the Big Pasture and put 'em where they used to be (she lost him right after 'you take the pickup').

"Don't get too close to that gate if it's surrounded by water because even in four-wheel drive you could bury this thing up to the hub-caps (she made a mental note to check behind the seat for a life jacket).

"On second thought, go through the Middle Pasture past the old schoolhouse to the windmill with the green gate panels. Then bring the heifers out that gate with the staple in it into the Big Pasture (Oh, no — the Staple Gate! Wonder Woman herself couldn't open that gate with her golden lasso and a come-a-long). Then you'll have a straight shot to the last gate where Gene bucked off the roan colt (in 1979), which leads to where the heifers used to be.

"I'm gonna take the four-wheeler and go through the other gate where the heifers were 'cause it's closer to the mineral feeder and I can check that windmill while I'm there and fill the feeder. See ya in a bit."

A bit passes.

"Where were you?" he asked. "I moved the heifers by myself and fixed another windmill. When you didn't show up I started lookin'. What are you doin' back here anyway? You could have come out the other gate. You were closer to it, ya know."

She took a deep breath and replied bravely, "I got the heifers through the Staple Gate, but it took so long to close it I turned the wrong way. I followed the road to the windmill we'd checked and realized I'd gone too far (not to mention that the heifers had disappeared). So I remembered what you'd told me: 'If you ever get lost in the Big Pasture, get up high, then you can see the fence. Go to the fence and follow it to a gate' (which is as useless a piece of information to someone like her as finding your way home by looking for moss growing on the north side of trees when you're lost in the woods).

"So I climbed this hill and dropped into a bull hole (buffalo waller for you Okies). The truck made 'that noise' and stopped ('that noise' that causes anyone who doesn't like hiking to break out in a cold sweat). I managed to back the truck out and come back the way I came till I found the Staple Gate, where I've been waiting for you to find me."

"Hmm," he says and loads the four-wheeler in the pickup and they start back to the house. He drives. As they bounce along the sandy track he puts his hand on her knee, and she rests her hand on his shoulder. The truck is still making "that noise," but it doesn't bother them.

They're pardners. Together they can handle anything.

On the Edge of Common Sense

By Baxter Black

Women who love cowboys

Illustration by Boots Reynolds

IT CAME as wonderful news that scientists had finally mapped the human genome. Now they know the arrangement of all the DNA that make up the cells in our bodies. Knowing what is right allows us to also know what is wrong, which can help delineate and subvert genetic defects. A momentous breakthrough, but it rang a small alarm bell in the back of my brain.

Most cowboy types like me never question how we wind up attracting a fairly decent type of woman. I was reminded of this when I attended the wedding of one of my good friends.

I have known him 20 years and love him like a brother, but I am intimately acquainted with his major flaws. Flaws that I discount, because I have the same ones. Yet, with the exception of falling in love with him, his new bride seemed an intelligent person.

All my life I have attracted these like-minded misfits. I mean characters you wouldn't have in your home on a holiday. And yet, they have all married or at least tempted women who are unexpectedly nice, smart, and, in every other respect, discerning humans.

I have concluded that their willingness to marry a "cowboy type" is the result of a genetic defect. One that blocks out the good judgment gene.

So you can see my concern. If this defect in her chromosomes was corrected, would she then be able to see our misguided priorities, like missing the birth of our first child because we had to go roping.

Or our belligerent stubbornness, when we insist that there is still gas in the tank even though the gauge says empty.

Or our uncouthness, like at supper when we insist on explaining the difficulties of replacing a uterine prolapse to our new in-laws, who are both Presbyterian ministers.

But as long as this defect remains intact in a certain number of females, we will always be able to begat little cowboys. And we are lucky that it is a sex-related trait. It is obviously a gender-specific genetic defect, isn't it?

Personally, I can't think of a single case where men have fallen in love with a woman with major character flaws.

We are genetically programmed to weigh all her assets and debits and make well-informed decisions about love and marriage, an area in which we are superior ... not to mention being very open-minded.

So, that's how it is, and I don't want to hear any more.

On The Edge Of Common Sense

By Baxter Black, D.V.M.

She Does the Books

Illustration by Mike Craig

This is my wife. She does the books;
 I do all the important stuff.
Like mend the fence and check the cows;
 she makes sure the income's enough.

To cover the cost of ranchin';
 she's tight as a new hatband.
I need to buy a new baler;
 she figgers out if we can.

I spend all day in the saddle;
 she's in the office all day,
Just talkin' with the SCS,
 or checkin' the price of hay.

Or dealin' with the accountants
 and keepin' the banker straight.
I might be cleanin' a ditch out,
 or hangin' a rusty gate.

She fills out all the blasted forms,
 the government makes us keep.
She reads those regulations till
 she's fightin' 'em in her sleep.

Me, I go to sleep a-dreamin'
 of bulls and barns and sales.
She's dreamin' the inventory
 or estimatin' bales.

She still finds time to bake a pie
 between her business deals.
And I keep busy all the time
 just greasin' squeaky wheels.

I told my wife that we should think
 'bout gettin a hired man.
Runnin' a ranch ain't easy—
 good managers need a plan.

She agreed that it weren't easy
 to manage and keep abreast.
"But, why," she asked, "get a hired man?
 I've already got the best."

On the Edge of Common Sense

By Baxter Black

Waiting for Daddy

"Mama, when's Daddy comin' home? Is it time to worry yet?"
"By supper, darlin'. Eat your Cheerios."
He rode out this morning early. Like he does 6 days a week.
I always make him tell me where he goes
'Specially when I know he's headed over on the canyon side
At least I know I'll have a place to start
So in case he doesn't come back I can hunt for him myself
Or go for help if I get faint of heart.

"Run and git your schoolbooks, kiddos! And be sure to wash yer hands."
"Aw Mama, do we have to school today?"
If it wasn't for home schooling I might lose what mind I've got
It helps to pass the daylight time away
And I know I shouldn't worry but I worry anyway
Who wouldn't, if they were in my shoes
I've been up those rocky canyons and I've seen those snaky trails
I know how quick a horse can blow a fuse.

"Mama, Cody said a swear word." "I did not." "Did too." "Did not."
"I only said Ring went to the commode."
Oh, thank God I've these children just to keep me occupied
But still I'm always lookin' down the road
All afternoon I've watched the sky. It's like I'm playing poker
You don't know how I fear an angry cloud
And the wind gives me the shivers. Never lets me drop my guard.
Nothin' like it whispers quite so loud.

"Mama, when's Daddy comin' home? Shouldn't he be home by now?
We wanna ride before it gets too dark."
And the hardest time for me I guess is now till 6 o'clock
I'm nervous till I hear the home dogs bark
But the kids are my salvation. 'Course, they wanna be like Dad
He saddles up their horse and lets 'em go
And I stand here by the window thinkin' 'here we go again'
But they're cowboyin', the only life they know.

"Mama, look! Oh, here comes Daddy. That's him trottin' up the road.
He's wavin', now he's comin' through the gate."
"See, I told you kids be patient, not to get your dander up . . ."
And learn to wait, and wait and wait and wait.

Illustration by Mike Craig

ON THE EDGE OF COMMON SENSE | BY BAXTER BLACK

Cowboys' Advice to the Lovelorn

I got a lesson a while back from three California cowboys, who were considering a sideline occupation; advice to the lovelorn. I should note that some people's conception of a "California cowboy" as a latte-drinking, Hollywood-primping, designer-chaps-wearing, buff, puff buckaroo doesn't describe these gentlemen. They had hard hands, a wary look and rolled their own. Some samples of their advice a' la Dear Abby, might go like this:

Dear Triplicating Cowpunchers,
What's the best way to get a guy to commit?
Signed, Desperately Seeking

Dear Desperately — Commit to what?

Dear Tumbleweed Triage,
Our first wedding anniversary is coming up soon, and I'd like to get a gift for my wonderful cowboy hubby that will be thoughtful, sweet and demonstrative of my love for him that will last through the ages.
Signed, Still Swooning

Dear Swooning — Beer is always a good choice.

Dear Tripe-Eating Triplets,
I'd like to marry my cowboy, Robert, and have proposed to him in a poem, which I can't quite finish. Can you help me? It begins:
"I'll marry you, I'm ready, Bob,
If you'll just get a _____."
Signed, Anxious in Oxnard

Dear Anxious — If Richard Petty was marketing corn byproducts, we could have been more helpful, but, sorry, nothing else comes to mind.

Dear Saddle Trio,
My wife wants a divorce but still insists on us going to a marriage counselor, so she can say she tried. What should I do?
Signed, In-the-Crosshairs

Dear Crosshairs – Change states.

Dear Triple Tie-Down Triad,
I'm a 22-year-old ex-model, now vice-president with a new Dodge dually, three-horse slant, ranchette with roping arena and four credit cards. How can I get my surfing boyfriend to pop the question?
Signed, Palomino Yearning

Dear Yearning — Kiss your surfing smoothie goodbye, and send a copy of your résumé, complete with a picture of the Dodge dually to: tritipcowboys@rightonbaby.com.

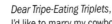

Dear Thundering Threesome,
In an effort to impress my cowboy significant other, I just completed a six-week course in international cuisine and want to impress him with a special intimate dinner in his honor. Any Suggestions?
Signed, The Cowgirl Cocinera

Dear Cocinera — Beer is always a good choice.

Dear Triangular Trailriders,
My cowboy has been out in the wagon, and I haven't seen him for six weeks. Any ideas for what I might wear for our first night back together?
Signed, Stars in her Eyes

Dear Stars — Barbecue sauce.

On the edge of common sense

By Baxter Black

Coming out

Illustration by
J.P. Rankin

THERE ARE few things more painful to watch than the "coming out" of a cowboy.

I had known Don for 25 years. Known his family, sat at his table, and leaned on him now and then. He was a good ranch manager in his day. Did things the cowboy way and was honest as a cedar post.

I recently ran into him and we had a warm reunion. "Whatcha doin' now?" I asked.

He sort of hemmed and hawed. "Oh, I been doin' a little day work for a fellow up the road."

"On a ranch?" I asked.

"Not exactly. ..."

"A feedyard deal?"

"Well, no. ..."

"Let me guess," I harassed him, "yer leadin' tourists around the desert on a bunch of ol' plugs and tellin' 'em what a great cowboy you were!" I laughed at my joke. He turned pale. I suddenly got embarrassed, "I was only kiddin'. I know you wouldn't ever. ..." His eyes began to well with tears.

"You mean?" I asked.

He nodded mournfully. "I'm wranglin' dudes."

I glanced around nervously, not wanting any of our cowboy friends to overhear.

"I just sort of fell into it," he snuffled and began to confess. I handed him my hanky. "We moved to town where my wife could get a good job. I tried sellin' western clothes, building saddles, even tried to be a movie extra, which is awful close to wranglin' dudes, then finally this carny kiddie ride guy offered me a job tendin' his dude string. The grandkids were back with us; we needed the money."

"It's not so bad," I said, patting his shoulder. "You'll get back with the cows sometime."

"No, I'm already a marked man. I've learned some yodeling tricks. They tip bigger if you tuck yer pants in your boot tops and wear a stampede string. I've even started writing cowboy poetry. I go by the name 'Sagebrush.' "

"Surely not!" I put my arm around him. It was an emotional moment.

"Yes," he said through the tears, "I even have names for the horses—Fury, Black Beauty, My Little Pony, Buttermilk. ..."

I stopped him. "They have clinics, ya know. There's one in Luverne, Minnesota. Not a tourist for miles. You can get back to basics—saddle, rope, cow."

"It's no use," he said, catching his breath and sighing. "It's just that ... I like it. They think I'm king of the cowboys! They like my stories. They think I'm a hero like John Wayne or Billy Crystal or Robert Redford."

"Why, they couldn't even pack your saddle," I snorted.

"I know," he said, "but we're all in show business."

I shook my head. "Sorry, ol' pal. Well, I'll see ya. I gotta go make some promo spots for my next appearance at the big western Art Fest and Boot and Spur Show."

JP RANKIN © 1999
THE CARTOON COWBOY

BY BAXTER BLACK, DVM

Friends

I WAS WALKING BACK TO THE HOUSE about 9:30 p.m. It was dark. Orion, the Seven Sisters, Taurus and Canis Major were blazin' away as I walked by a beautiful handmade bird feeder, complete with water tower, laurel branches and a copper-roofed cabin. Dan made it for me the year before he died.

"Evenin', Dan," I said as I passed it by.

"Howdy, Wayne," I said as I scraped my boots on the handmade, horseshoe foot-scraper. "Thanks."

That afternoon, I had put on a 10-year-old pair of Carhartt overalls Andy had given me when he bought a new pair; he is a better dresser than I and has always tried to class up my act.

"Thanks Andy.

"And, Larry, thanks for this hat."

There was snow on my 2-year-old Suburban this morning. I've had it a month. Red got a new one, and I always buy his trade-ins. They usually need new brakes or transmission work. But it's worth the money.

"Thanks, Red."

We checked the heifers this morning. My good horse I got from Sonny, my bit from Chuck, and my saddle from Roger; they give me good deals. I'm trying to live up to their expectations. One of the heifers in the bunch is the daughter of a cow Gerald traded when he left the ranch.

"Thanks, boys."

My dog went along. Mary had raised him, and Jeb showed me how to make him a better stock dog.

"Thanks."

I can't walk through the house or out to the corrals without tripping over someone's contribution to my good life—Grandpa Tommy's eight-foot table, Jack's gate, Dick's molasses tank, Grandpa Landers' Regulator clock, Butch's eight-track studio board, Warner's jaguar photo, Ace's cartoons, Mother's paintings on the wall, Chris' furniture, Ron's tapaderos, Phyllis' caned chairs, Pinto's subscription to a favorite publication—friends, mostly, who have taken the time to do something special.

More properly, it's people who have penetrated my marrow, and help me remember how lucky I am. For me, it's the people whose names I remember.

I sent a book to an old partner now living in a nursing home. He can't remember me anymore, but I know him. Forty years ago, he gave me a beautiful hunting knife. It had a flexible blade. Through the years I lost it or wore it out; who knows? But there is a deer head hanging above my piano that came off his ranch.

When I go see him next time, he probably won't know me, but I'll tell him about the hunting knife and the deer head on my wall. I'll tell Billy what a blessing it has been to have him in my life. I'll honor him.

Couldn't hurt. 🐴

BAXTER BLACK

ON THE EDGE OF COMMON SENSE

The Rest of Us

He used to break horses, he used to herd sheep,
He worked in a feedlot a while.
He grew up a'dreamin' he'd buy him a ranch
And raise horses and cattle in style.

But time pulled a fast one, life took a turn,
Dreams pulled the wool o'er his eyes,
'Cause it takes more than wishin' and workin' all day
To buy you a ranch and survive.

So now he sells saddles, or vaccine, or seed,
Or writes for the Livestock Gazette,
Doin' whatever it takes to stay close
To the land that he'll never get.

In ag economics or ranch real estate,
In his hat and his boots and his gloves,
Collectin' his check as he goes down the road
From the folks that he wishes he was.

Hell, he knows he's lucky to just have a job
That lets him stay close to his roots.
He may never own the ranch of his dreams
But at least he can pay for his boots.

Illustration by Wally Badgett

On the Edge of Common Sense

By Baxter Black

Water

Illustration by Don Gill

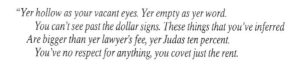

"Yer hollow as your vacant eyes. Yer empty as yer word.
You can't see past the dollar signs. These things that you've inferred
Are bigger than yer lawyer's fee, yer Judas ten percent.
You've no respect for anything, you covet just the rent.

"T he big boy land developers hired them a worn out hack
To go and buy the water rights off farmers down the track.
"Just pay 'em anything they ask. Hell, any price on earth.
Those farmers haven't got a clue of what it's really worth."

Go back to your rich puppeteers who've never broke a sweat.
Who ride in when the battle's done and use their bayonet
To finish off the wounded brave and pick their pockets clean
Then sell their spoils to innocents to keep their cities green.

"Them's fightin' words," the farmer said. *"This water ain't for sale.*
It's all that keeps this place alive. Without it crops would fail."
The lawyer sorta laughed it off. "We'll get it anyway.
The cities need it all to grow. You can't stand in their way.

Explain to them the difference between value and price.
The value isn't worth what is paid, it's what is sacrificed
That gives it worth. It's measured in the turns around a field,
In families and community, in broken bonds and healed.

It's progress, you should know by now you can't hold back the flood."
"There's lifetimes given to this land. The water's in their blood."
"Old man that's ancient history, besides we'll make you rich.
Just name yer price, you'll have it. It's nothin' but a ditch."

In barns burnt down and harvest lost and kids gone off to war.
Explain to them it's measured in grooves worn in your soul . . . or,
In depths of neighbor's breaking hearts when someone's lost a wife,
And that you can't just set a price on someone's way of life.

> ## On the Edge of Common Sense

BY **BAXTER BLACK, DVM**

The Last Man

THEY ARE SUBDIVIDING the section that borders me. Since the time the Spanish explorers introduced cattle into my valley in the 1600s, there have been livestock on that piece of ground.

Last week, I saddled up and rode that pasture again. Its mesquite arroyos and grassy ridges are speckled with ocotillo. I was just looking to see how close to the canyon rim the houses were planned. Right to the edge.

The south fence was pushed over. Piles of uprooted mesquite huddled, feet to the sun. Dug up barrel cacti squatted in rows, loose dirt kicked over their roots. Wooden survey stakes stood like skinny tombstones, crude numbers scrawled on their faces. The big mesquite shade tree where the cows gathered to gossip was trimmed lopsided like an old man with a stroke, its dignity lost.

My horse knew the old trail. I dismounted to stand upright an ocotillo that had been avalanched by the bulldozer. Back in the saddle, I gave the ground one last look; the mountains that it had known all its life, the river in the valley that had received its runoff for thousands of years. They had kept each other company for a long time.

I had run cows up here for five years. A very short time in its three- or four hundred years as a ranch, but I would be the very last man to punch a cow on this sacred ground.

I have had some interesting firsts: first man to get a ticket on Peña Boulevard, the road from Denver to the city's new airport; first person to ride a horse on stage in the Elko auditorium; first person to spend the night in the Holiday Inn in Sheridan, Wyoming. I had a spectacular hat trick one year when I got a ticket for speeding in Texas, for going too slow in California, and for passing a policeman on a double yellow line in New Mexico. Other than those sterling accomplishments, I've puttered along like most folks—head down, nose to the grindstone, shoulder to the wheel, workin' my way through life.

But my personal best to date, I realized, settin' on that pretty piece of rangeland that had been consecrated by cowboys, cows and Coronado, is to be the last man to punch a cow on its fertile, fragile skin. So, bring on the cement boys, paint her face, Botox her wrinkles and pave her veins till she pings like a floozy. I knew her when, and ya can't take that away from me. 🐎

On the Edge of Common Sense

By Baxter Black

Nature's Logic

Illustration by J.P. Rankin

I WAS marveling at my horses' tails as they stood around in the shade. A perfect fly-shooing machine.

Then I wondered ... if it's so perfect, why doesn't a cow have a tail like a horse? The answer was obvious. A cow pie is usually much looser, more liquid than a road apple. If a cow had a horse's tail it would always be a stiff and sticky mess, unless a cow could preen and lick itself like a cat, which, of course, it can't.

It's the same difference between people with moustaches and people without them.

Evolution has predestined that the hair lippers are much neater eaters than the bare lippers (or should that be hirsute and baresuit?), or at least more prone to personal grooming. You may have noticed the moustachioed cowboys constantly fondling and stroking their facial hair — just survival of the fittest.

This continuing analogy applies to women's feet and frequency of marriages. Observation: In the last 40 years, the size of the average woman's foot has grown 2 sizes. Women's fashions use to lean toward sleek, pointed foot wear ... a graceful extension of the curvaceous calf, delicate ankle, and dainty foot.

Then, women's feet began to grow. Attempts to cram a size 11 triple A into a bullet-shaped shoe led observers to imagine giraffes in giant elf shoes or Admiral Perry cross-country skiing the Arctic wasteland.

And the number of marriages per person has increased considerably in conjunction with increase in foot size. Obviously a direct result of the female of the species being easier to track.

But back to the horse's tail. Its simplicity of design and utility of function has inspired many copycats in nature. Teenage girls wear their hair back in a ponytail and coordinate their swishing with gum popping and nasty gossip.

Not to mention the German shepherd, kite flying, or the landing parachute on the tail of a Russian bomber.

And every spring we see the ultimate adaptation of that equine appendage. Millions of new graduates standing in robes facing their futures, eyes glazed, palms sweating, and yet virtually fly-free, thanks to the tassel. Wave on eohippus. We are forever indebted.

JPRANKIN©2001
"THE CARTOON COWBOY"
cowboyartisans.com

On the edge of common sense

By Baxter Black

Carhartt cowboy

MR. MOSES remarked the other day he'd received a catalog in the mail from a western clothing outfit. He wasn't sure who the outfit catered to, but the name "Long Island" seemed to stick in his mind. The photo on the front had burned an image into his brain. A male model stood in cowboy posture, a Clint Eastwood steely-eyed glare glinting from beneath the brim of his Zorro hat.

It appeared that a moth had eaten the collar of his shirt.

He wore a duster that was sort of a cross between Jim Bridger's old trapping coat and Santa Anna's parade uniform. Mr. Moses guessed it weighed more than a wet hallway carpet. There was an odd collection of gold chains, buttons, military pins, silver boot toe tips, training spurs, and epaulettes decorating his wardrobe. He looked like a Filipino cabbie just returned from a Rotarian's convention.

Mr. Moses imaged himself dressed like the cowboy on the cover of the catalog, jangling out to feed the cows and break ice. Him hangin' his giant rowel and jingle-bob on the twine as he kicked a bale off the back of the flatbed. Being jerked flat into the muddy rut, cows tromping giant footprints on the tail of his coat, the dog running off with his pancake hat. Then rising, sodden, and trudging off rattling and clanging like a Moroccan bride with a limp.

"Shoot," he said, "I couldn't even walk up to a horse dressed like that."

Mr. Moses considers himself a Carhartt cowboy. For those of you who live in the tropics, Carhartts are warm, insulated canvas overalls with more zippers than a Hell's Angel's loincloth.

Carhartts, ear flaps, and LaCrosse five-buckle overshoes. Real cowboy winter wear. Granted, it limits your mobility. You'd have to get undressed to mount yer horse. You can't hear much other than the diesel, but a cowboy can get the job done.

Could be the cowboy on the catalog cover measures his time in the winter by the bottles of brandy he goes through, lacing his evening café au lait, or possibly the edge of the sun rays on the floor of his glassed-in sun room. Certainly it would not be the amount of mud built up in the wheel wells of his Lexus.

Mr. Moses has his own way of judging the length of winter. He says he keeps track by watchin' the pile of ice that accumulates next to the stock tank.

Spoken like a true Carhartt cowboy.

Illustration by Kevin Cordtz

CORDTZ 99

BAXTER BLACK

ON THE EDGE OF COMMON SENSE

CAMP COOKIE

He's the tumbleweed chef and rides with the wagon
ahead of the thunderin' herd.
His pots and pans clack like a diamondback's rattle,
he growls or he don't say a word.

His face is a roadmap. Looks like a carcass
hung too many days in the sun.
He smells like a mule and cooks with a shovel
and his fly is always undone.

The riders kin tell when he's in the kitchen—
the buzzards all come into view.
He spits in the pan and shaves in the taters
and clips his toenails in the stew.

His gunpowder biscuits explode in the fire;
his beans explode in yer bowel.
His medda lark souffle is hard on the belly;
they say it tastes 'bout like a owl.

His coffee's so rank a housefly won't touch it,
even buckshot floats in the slop.
You don't pour a cup, you twist off a swaller,
then chew a sip offa the top.

Now, cowboys are tough guys who face death each day
in blizzards or stampedes or storms.
They ride them bad horses and sleep with the snakes
and duel with the hooves and the horns.

But many a cowboy who follered the wagon
has joined the "last roundup club."
Not from Indians, gunfights, or even bad whiskey,
but from eatin' Camp Cookie's grub.

Illustration by
Boots Reynolds

On the Edge of Common Sense   BY **BAXTER BLACK, DVM**

Reality Shows on the Farm

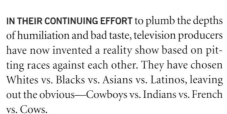

IN THEIR CONTINUING EFFORT to plumb the depths of humiliation and bad taste, television producers have now invented a reality show based on pitting races against each other. They have chosen Whites vs. Blacks vs. Asians vs. Latinos, leaving out the obvious—Cowboys vs. Indians vs. French vs. Cows.

I can see spin-offs in the agricultural world: **Hereford Breeders vs. Angus Breeders**. It would be billed as "Cancer Eye vs. Prolapsed Sheath!" Contestants would be forced to mouth, preg-check and cull purebred look-alikes from the Nacogdoches sale barn, and the audience would pick the winner.

Horse People vs. Mule People: The Overconfident vs. the True Believers! This reality show would force mule people to beat horse people in every possible contest. Then, the horse people would have to try to explain why the horse really won.

Stock-Dog Border Collies vs. City-Park Border Collies: Sheep Police vs. Frisbee Catchers! Sheep men would order their Border Collies to herd ducks, old ewes, baby calves, kindergarten classes or intransigent Pomeranians through an intricate obstacle course to display their natural ability and intelligence. City Border Collies would respond by jumping hurdles, catching balls and running through culverts, displaying their usefulness in case of a presidentially declared state of hurdle, ball and culvert emergency!

House Cats vs. Barn Cats: Kitty Litter vs. Mouse-Eating Machines! House cats will make a show of their household superiority by demonstrating their ability to completely dominate the humans who wait on them hand and paw. Points will be scored on such traits as personality, appetite, sleeping on best furniture, shedding and disdain.

This is one farm reality show that probably wouldn't work because there's no way to catch a barn cat!

And … my last suggestion for an agricultural reality-survival show: **Large-Animal Veterinarian vs. Small-Animal Veterinarian**. The loser will be determined by how many times during an eight-week period each tries to spay a tomcat or pregnancy-check a steer!

I love writing this column! 🐎

Jack and His Dog Bed

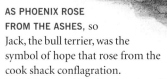

AS PHOENIX ROSE FROM THE ASHES, so Jack, the bull terrier, was the symbol of hope that rose from the cook shack conflagration.

Jack was past his prime, but though hard of hearing and losing his sight, he still continued to make the winter trip to Walker's camp in the Rocky Mountains of Colorado. In spite of the cold he slept outside, near the cooking fire, in his own dog bed.

The night the camp caught fire, it was harrowing. Most of the supplies were lost, plus rifles, saddles, tack and years' worth of personal treasures. The next morning, the fire had burned itself out. In the deep ashes lay the metal skeletons of tools, utensils, firearms and hardware. Jack had survived.

Walker spent most of the morning gathering salvageables and sifting memories. He loaded the horses in the trailer, Jack in the bed of the pickup, and slid and slipped down the muddy track to Highway 50. There, he got out to check his load and saw that Jack had abandoned ship.

The weather was below freezing, the dog was old, and it was two miles back to the camp on top of the mountain. Walker considered, like most of us would, the consequences of abandoning Jack, and, like most of us, he couldn't. He backtracked, searched for five hours and then had to make the agonizing decision to leave without him. Home was 600 miles away in Arizona.

That night, Walker called his Colorado neighbor, John, to report the fire and Jack's disappearance. Two days later, John worked his way back through bad winter weather to the site of the fire. To his amazement, he found a tunnel in the ashes and snow. Jack had returned to the camp, burrowed in and found his dog bed. He planned to hibernate, John guessed.

John hauled Jack back home to his ranch house and put him up in the mud room, on a door mat. By the next morning, Jack had run away again. John made the long trip back to the burned camp. No Jack. Two days later, another neighbor called to inquire if anybody had lost a grumpy, snuffling, old gray dog. John was relieved. It turns out that Jack had left in search of better quarters. He had somehow gotten inside the neighbor's house, found a dog bed and claimed it for his own, much to the consternation of the resident poodle.

"He even ate my Kibbles and used the cat's sandbox!" the poodle was heard to say. "Now my bed is soaked in drool, covered with dog hair and smells like barbecued goat."

Jack, never one take offense, snuggled down and slept through it all. 🐎

On the Edge of Common Sense

By Baxter Black

Cowboy Vocabulary Misconceptions

Illustration by Don Gill

THIS COLUMN has an agricultural-cowboy slant. However, I am aware that urban people ("gentile," I call them) read it as well. So when I lapse into my "cowboy vocabulary," I appreciate that some of my meaning could be unclear. Listed are some common misconceptions:

Statement: "My whole flock has keds."
Misinterpretation: Sheep are now endorsing tennis shoes.

Statement: "I'm looking to buy some replacement heifers but I want only polled cattle."
Misinterpretation: His cows are being interviewed by George Gallup.

Statement: "I'm going to a gaited-horse show."
Misinterpretation: A horse performance being held in an exclusive residential area.

Statement: "I work in a hog confinement facility."
Misinterpretation: She teaches classes in the campus jail at University of Arkansas.

Statement: "I prefer the Tarentaise over the Piedmontese."
Misinterpretation: He is picky about cheese.

Statement: "They've had a lot of blowouts at the turkey farm this year."
Misinterpretation: Sounds like they better change tire dealers.

Statement: "This mule is just a little owly."
Misinterpretation: His ears stick up? He's wise beyond his species limitation? No, wait, he looks like Benjamin Franklin or Wilford Brimley?

Statement: "Do you know where I could get a bosal, romal and some tapaderas?"
Misinterpretation: I'd suggest someplace that served Mexican food.

Statement: "I heard that Speed Williams and Rich Skelton got one down in five flat."
Misinterpretation: Must be a couple of quick anesthesiologists.

Statement: "I heard Texas has now gotten Brucellosis-free."
Misinterpretation: I assume Bruce, who is of Greek origin, finally got a good lawyer.

Statement: "The beef check-off has gone up to a dollar."
Misinterpretation: Not a bad price for a Russian sandwich. I know the Veal Solginetzen and the Chicken Zhavago are twice that much.

Statement: "You don't have to be a genius to see the team pulls to the left."
Misinterpretation: Whoever they are were not satisfied with the election results.

Statement: "I believe that Debouillet has blue bag."
Misinterpretation: She's taken to wearing French fashion accessories.

Statement: "That horse won't break out of a canter."
Misinterpretation: Then that's what I'd keep him in. Beats tyin' him to a post.

Statement: "She's wormed, fresh offa wheat grass and showin' a little ear."
Misinterpretation: A modest stripper on an organic diet has swallowed her chewing tobacco.

Statement: "You can stick a fork in me."
Misinterpretation: He's done. 🐎

ON THE EDGE OF COMMON SENSE | BY BAXTER BLACK

The Cowboy's Excuse: I Messed Up

Even when you have good intentions, it's possible to make a complete wreck of the situation. It's normal to cast about for something to blame: "The horse ducked his head." "I hit a pothole." "I thought it said two pounds!" "She was leaning on me." "The light was bad." "I always do it that way!"

As my disasters accumulated through the years, I've finally realized that sometimes I just mess up. It's the truth, and who can argue with it?

Recently I received a note that a wife of a friend of mine wasn't long for this world. She'd been suffering a prolonged illness, and her time was nigh. I'd become close to this friend and his brother. With a heavy heart, I wrote a note to the couple thanking them for their inspiration. I offered the consolation they'd be together in heaven. I mailed it.

A week later I received word that Helen (not her real name) had passed away. "Helen?" I said. "I thought it was Ruth that died!" I was mortified. I called both brothers,

apologizing profusely for my erroneous, insensitive error. They were gracious, but I don't think I'll be invited to their next family reunion. How can I live with myself, you ask? I look myself in the eye and say, "Cowboy, ya just messed up."

James (not his real name) is like that. Sometimes things start out perfectly fine. He means well, everything's going according to plan and then, WHAM! Like the time he was riding down main street in his beautiful, Colorado high-mountain hometown.

The proprietor of a local establishment hollered at James to ride his horse on in. What a great idea! It's not often a cowboy gets that invitation, so he spurred his pony up the steps, through the door and up to the bar. The tourists loved it! They took pictures, and bought James and his horse a beer or three. He departed with a wave and galloped out in the street. It struck him that it was such a good idea, he should

just do it again. So he did, next door. But his reception at the North Park Fidelity Bank wasn't nearly as warm. He was summarily arrested and jailed on a D.U.I., making a deposit under the influence.

Another day he was pushing a big ornery bull down the trail from Pole Mountain. The bull sulled up and got on the fight. James tried whacking him with the tail of his rope; then, to even up the odds, James pulled a pair of pliers from his holster and tied them to the end of his rope to give it more heft. It worked. The bull charged him, tipped over his horse, pinning James underneath.

When Blaine rode up on them, the bull was standing on the horse's neck, which was on top of James, who was ferociously whacking the bull on the nose with a set of pliers that didn't weigh much more than a Teflon spatula.

"What happened?" asked Blaine after he rescued his pardner.

"Oh, nothing," said James. "I just messed up." 🐎

The Cowboy's Document of Contrition

WHEREAS **THE AVERAGE COWBOY** is a person of good intentions, generous to a fault and kind to women, children and animals; and *Whereas* said cowboy is often in the right place at the wrong time and driven by an overdeveloped sense of chivalry, bravado or tradition; and *Whereas* you may frequently find said cowboy at the center of many a controversial, embarrassing or blatantly stupid miscarriage of sanity; this form is offered as a document through which said cowboy acknowledges his participation in some grievous social, marital, work-related, or animal-inspired or tequila-afflicted misbehavior.

Offender, please circle one or more of these excuses:

1. I freely admit that I lost control of
   a) my mouth
   b) my good dog
   c) the balloons full of beer I was juggling.

2. I now realize that
   a) it was not as funny as I thought
   b) you didn't have fire (flood) insurance
   c) weed-eaters are not the proper way to
      slice cheesecake.

3. It is true that
   a) I didn't know your uncle had a pacemaker when I
      handed him the Hotshot
   b) you should avoid microwaving paint-gun balls
   c) skeet shooting should be done outdoors.

4. I will not be surprised to know that my hosts
   a) really expected more mature behavior
   b) have written me out of the will
   c) have filed suit to recover the cost of repairing
      the bass boat I fired up in the yard and the gazebo
      I wiped out with it.

5. What I want the offendee(s) to know, in my defense, is
   a) I am fully aware of the damage I have done to our
      relationship, the landscaping and the parrot cage, and
      I humbly apologize
   b) I messed up. I'm sorry I did. I didn't mean to wreck
      (your party, our date, your grandmother's Bowflex).
      Sometimes I just get carried away, and if you give me
      one more chance, I promise I'll try to do better.
   c) I am unable to remember what happened, but if the
      DNA matches, I take complete responsibility

(Print Name Here) _____

❯ On the Edge of Common Sense

BY **BAXTER BLACK, DVM**

One of the Cowboy Days

IT'S THE KIND OF DAY every cowboy dreams of. Almost makes you wish they weren't numbered. When the desert is green, it's like Wyoming when the wind's not blowing, or a sunny winter day in Ohio.

Still supposed to be hot today, but we've got morning cloud cover so at 8:30 it's not bad.

Two days ago, we dumped a handful of cows in this canyon pasture. They haven't found the water yet, so our job this morning is to push 'em back to the water trap and start over. First trick, of course, is to find 'em. Not as simple as it is in some places. From the top of a ridgeline, the big bosques of mesquite amongst the ridges and arroyos look like green lakes surrounded by sandy hills and rocky fjords.

I always empathized with those cowmen in Missouri and elsewhere who run cows in the woods. Especially since they don't even have any high ground to ride up on to take a look!

Lo and behold, there was a flash of white in the sea of mesquite green—maybe the white cow. I'd like to say a Charolais, but I suspect she's not purebred. The white spot disappears but we've got their location. This saves us riding clear to the backside.

The monsoon rains have been plentiful, grass is abundant, and though it's still green it's beginning to go to seed. Down in the brush where the mesquite, cat claw and white thorn rake at our leggings, we ride as the horses pick their way like pole-bending porpoises.

The wild flowers are rioting, so fragile they melt in your hand: yellow daisies, orange poppies, delicate white blossoms with petals no bigger than a grain of rice, purple morning glories, little blue cornets, giant ivory jimsonweed trombones. And starring in its full bloom, the bulbous, porkypinish barrel cacti with their slashes of deep red that gleam as your eyes constantly scan for tracks and cows.

Even the light green- and rust-colored lichens decorating the rocks are reveling in the day. Jackrabbits are fat and the deer are everywhere you look. All the four-footed grazers and browsers are enjoying the heavy mesquite bean crop, and the giant stalks of many century plants have been gnawed to a ragged stump.

I don't know if the deer, coyotes or javelina, cow dogs or hawks, rattlesnakes, Gila monsters, quail, mountain lions or cows appreciate what a glorious day this is, but I know one cowboy who understands this is as good as it gets. 🐎

HOLIDAYS

It was the night before Christmas and Rudolph was lame!

Western Horseman always does my Christmas poems up big! Friend and Cowboy Artists of America's one and only Herb Mignery has illustrated most of them.

I've always had the good sense to have my books illustrated. The right picture can draw attention to a poem, or away from it! Either way can be positive if it helps to sell a book!

Many of my Christmas stories are frivolous . . . funny. They are animal stories. Animals can be funny in their own right: horses yawning, cows scratching, or sheep chuckling at you. But when we add an elk whose antlers are crossed, cows who lead secret lives like women in bowling leagues, and plastic sleeves hung up around the barn on Christmas Eve, you get a peek into the sometimes bizarre thought processes that possess cowboy poets on occasion.

Other of my stories and poems lend a "cowboy's view" of Christ, which also, as usual, features animals.

Christmas is a time of respect, reverence, family, love, big eating, friends and giving. It is also like any other day in the horse barn or at the corrals. We who have the responsibility for God's creatures rise before the others, go feed, break ice and do the chores before we join the celebration. These simple acts, repeated unending since horse and man took on the cow, define us and our place in the giant scheme of things.

It's where I belong, with people like that.

Little Christmas Cowboy

By Baxter Black

Illustration by Herb Mignery

He got his first horse at Christmas this year
  from good ol' Uncle Stephen.
For wrangler-in-charge, he looked pretty young
  but looks can be deceivin'.

He topped out his bronc 'fore cook lit the fire
  with lots of loud ty-yi'-in'.
And if he laid off or slighted the horse
  it weren't for lack of tryin'.

He rope broke him quick and taught him to back
  and hold tight any bad actor.
No critter escaped the reach of his loop;
  Pooh, Big Bird, or the tractor.

They covered the range from sofa to rug
  and ruled the carpet nation.
The dog and the cat gave him wide berth,
  such was his reputation.

Sometimes he would take his quiver and bow
  and wear a turkey feather.
"Me Indie," he'd say and chase buffalo.
  The plains went on forever.

When Sonny would buck, and he could sure buck,
  the kid might come unscated.
"Me rodeo, Dad," then get right back on,
  scuffed up but undefeated.

Last night after chuck he readied for bed
  but since he'd not unsaddled
He patted his horse and asked, "Okay, Dad,
  me, Sonny, check the cattle?"

I mighta been green but I could detect
  a sucker play unfoldin'.
Just any excuse so he could stay up,
  each second saved was golden.

"Sure, git on yer horse," I prompted the kid.
  He sorta hesitated.
He wasn't quite dressed to mount up and ride,
  his inner mind debated.

He gathered his rope and steadied the horse
  then looked back for permission.
The boss held his gaze, then gave him a nod.
  He swung into position.

He let out a whoop and rode off to give
  the herd a quick inspection.
To be a top hand, you go by the rules,
  the height of circumspection.

He'd already learned that young buckaroos
  must check in with their mamas,
'Cause she'd always said that real cowboys
  don't ride in their pajamas. 🐴

What's Christmas to a Cow?

By Baxter Black
Illustration by Herb Mignery

I know you've prob'ly asked yourself,
    what's Christmas to a cow?
You've not? Well maybe, just perchance
    I've got you thinking now.
When we march out on Christmas morn
    like nothin's goin' on,
Has Yuletide struck the night before
    and disappeared by dawn?
Were plastic sleeves a'hangin' up
    around the calvin' shed?
Did visions of molasses blocks
    cavort inside her head?
And did she lay awake all night
    tensed up, anticipating
Or, in excitement, milk her bed
    by accident, while waiting?

Do cows pretend to be just cows,
    devoid of all intrigues
But really lead a secret life
    like women's bowling leagues?
Did we just miss the mistletoe;
    did all the clues elude us?
Does she believe in Santa Claus
    or just Santa Gertrudis?
And if we looked would we see sign
    of reindeer in the pen,
Or would we just convince ourselves
    the goat got out again?
And after we'd all gone to bed
    would they join in a hymn?
And sing that little manger song
    they learned in Bethlehem?

I guess that it don't matter much
    if cows believe or not.
We'll fork her out a flake of hay
    and head back in a trot
To celebrate our Christmas Day
    and all that we espouse.
And when we say our dinner grace
    we'll thank Him for the cows,
For the livelihood they give us
    and life we get to share.
But do the cows have Christmas cheer—
    who knows, but just beware
If you see chicken tracks among
    the straw and drying chips,
You'd better check suspicious cows
    for eggnog on their lips.

How Do You Know It's Christmas?

By Baxter Black

Illustration by Herb Mignery

So, how do you know it's Christmas?

'Cause the sheep can always tell.
They follow a little tradition and have for quite a spell.
On Christmas Eve around midnight, the sheep, wherever they are,
All rise in quiet unison and fixate on a star.
And from their stirring comes a sound, a chuckling Tra, La, La
That weaves and builds itself into a soft, melodious BAA
Which carries like a dove's lament when nights are very still,
As if they're calling for someone beyond a yonder hill.

The legend herds passed on down attributes this tradition
To one late night in Bethlehem. A heavenly petition
Wherein a host of angels came and lured them with a song.
The herders left in haste, they say, and stayed gone all night long.
Well, sheep don't do too well alone. They've never comprehended
That on that night they waited up, the world was upended.

So, now when daylight shortens up and nights get long and cold
I make my check at midnight like we've done since days of old.
And if I find the flock intent and standing all around,
I listen for the heavenly host above their throaty sound
And scan the dim horizon in an effort to discern
The sign the sheep are seeking, that their shepherds will return.
And I am but a watchman in this drama that replays
Around the earth this time of year, and so I stand and gaze.
And though I see no special star or hear no sweet noel,
I know it must be Christmas, 'cause the sheep can always tell. 🐴

Is There Really a Santa Claus?

By Baxter Black

Illustration by Herb Mignery

Dad, is there really a Santa Claus?"

Why do you ask?

"Jason's brother said there isn't. He's in the sixth grade."

What do you think?

"I think there is … but how does he know what I want for Christmas?"

You write out a list and send it to him, don't you?

"Yes, but if every kid does it, how does he ever read them all?"

Maybe the moms and dads help Santa get some stuff.

"Like if he runs out of Legos at the North Pole they can just get them at Kmart?"

Maybe that's how it works sometimes.

"Or maybe he's just too busy to make them all himself."

I do know moms and dads can tell Santy if the boys and girls have been good for goodness sakes and have not been selfish and know the real meaning of Christmas.

"I do. About Jesus being born and Mary and Joseph and the manger."

And how it is better to give than to receive.

"I always put out cookies and milk for Santa. That's a gift."

I think it's more like giving to others.

"To Tio Bob and Aunt Tamara and the cousins?"

And other kids who aren't as lucky as you are.

"Kind of like us being Santa's helpers?"

Yeah, that's a good way to look at it.

"So how does he find everybody?"

He must have a map of the world or just know the way.

"I'll bet the reindeer know the way just like Sony and Coyote know the way home after we're done riding."

Or maybe Santa just has a couple good dogs who ride in the sleigh. They could help him get home too.

"Like Hattie and Pancho. So, do you think I'll get an Arctic Lego Set for Christmas?"

I've already got it.

"Dad, do you believe in Santa Claus?"

Yep. If you're smart, you'll always believe in Santa Claus.

The Reindeer Flu

By Baxter Black  Illustration by Herb Mignery

You remember that Christmas a few years ago
  When you waited all night for ol' Santy to show
Well, I heard the reason and it just might be true
  The whole bunch came down with the dang reindeer flu

The cowboy elves had been busy all day
  A-doctorin' Donner and scatterin' hay
Dancer and Prancer were febrile and snotty
  Comet and Cupid went constantly potty

Hallucinatory dementia was rampant
  Why, Blitzen imagined that he was Jed Clampett
Dasher got schizo and thought he was Trigger
  While Vixen's obsessions got bigger and bigger

By noon Santy knew he should find substitutes
  So the cowboy elves went out searching recruits
They scoured the Arctic for suitable prey
  And brought them together to hook to the sleigh

When Santy climbed up it was like a bad dream
  He stared down the lines at the substitute team
A bull moose as old as the planks on the ark
  With a head as big as a hammerhead shark
Stood hitched by a cow, Mrs. Santy's of course
  Then next in the tugs was a Clydesdale horse

He was paired with an elk whose antlers were crossed
  An ostrich, a walrus, an old albatross
Were harnessed in line but the last volunteer
  Was a blue heeler dog with only one ear

The cowboy elves gave a push to the sled
  As Santy rared back, cracked his whip, then he said
"On Cleo, on Leo, on Lefty and Jake,
  On Morphus, Redondo, on Lupe and Snake . . ."
Smoke from the runners cut tracks in the snow
  The team headed south, but, where else could they go?

They started back East 'cause it got dark there first
  And their luck, which was bad, got progressively worse
By the time they hit Kansas the tugs had gone slack
  And all but the dog was now ridin' in back

Santy was desperate. What on earth could he do?
  When the lights of an airport hove into his view
Did they make it? You betcha, but there hangs the tale
  Of how, on that Christmas they stayed on the trail

A man in Alaska said right after dawn
  A low flying object passed over his lawn
He ran to the window and threw up the sash
  And heard someone shouting, "Fer Pete's sake, don't crash!

On Budget, on Thrifty, look out Alamo
  I didn't take out insurance, you know
And you, Number Two, try harder, yer Avis
  On Dollar, on Hertz, Rent-a-Wreck, you can save us

An extra day's charge if we make it by nine
  Though the drop-off will cost us a bundle this time
Merry Christmas," yelled Santy, but he was all smiles
  'Cause at least he'd signed up for unlimited miles

So that's how it happened as best I recall
  When it looked like that Christmas might not come at all
And the truth of the matter, we all owe a cheer
  To the Wichita office of Rent-a-Reindeer

Joe and Maria

The First Christmas...cowboy style.

By Baxter Black • Illustration by Herb Mignery

NOW I 'spect most of you cowboys have heard the story 'bout Christmas. How it came to be an' all, but I wanna 'splain it so y'all kin understand.

It started with this cowboy named Joe. He'd married a girl named Maria. Times was hard in them days. They's down to the crumbly jerky and one ol' paint gelding named Duke. To top it off, Maria was in the family way.

They'd been ridin' several days, with Joe mostly walkin'. They camped on the trail, and Maria was gettin' tired an' ornery. Late one night, December 24, I think, they spotted the lights of a little burg. It was a welcome sight 'cause the weather'd turned coolish.

There was only one hotel in town, and Joe offered to chop wood or wash dishes for a room, but they were full up. The clerk said they could lay out their rolls in the livery stable. Git 'em outta the wind, anyway.

So Joe built 'em a nest in one of the stalls and went out to rustle up some grub. When he came back, Maria was fixin' to have that baby. Well, Joe panicked.

He laid out his slicker, fluffed up the straw, and ran down the street lookin' for a doc. By the time he got back, Maria'd done had that baby. It was a boy. She had him wiped off an' wrapped up in Joe's extra long john shirt.

Joe was proud, and Maria was already talkin' baby talk to the little one. They discussed what to call him. Joe wouldn't have minded if they'd named him Joe Jr., but Maria wanted to call him Jesus. A promise she'd made before Joe knew her.

Maria was tuckered. Jesus was sleepin' like a baby, and Joe was tickin' like a $2 watch. Fatherhood had hit him like a bag of loose salt! Just then he heard singin'.

In through the door come six Mexican sheepherders. They gathered around the baby and said he sure looked good. "*Niño especial,*" they said. Then they laid out some tortillas and commenced to visit.

Suddenly three fellas rode right into the livery. There was two Indian braves and a black cavalry scout. They told Joe that they'd had a vision and followed a star right to this very spot.

Joe said, "No kiddin'?"

"Shore nuf," they said. This was a special baby. He'd be a chief someday. This was good news to Joe. Not only that, they'd brought three buffalo hides, two handmade blankets, and a little poke of gold dust, which they gave to Joe to use for the baby.

Joe and Maria were overwhelmed. One of the herders tied together a little crib. He packed the bottom with straw and laid a sheepskin over it. Maria laid baby Jesus in it, and He never woke, just gurgled and smiled.

Then the whole bunch of 'em stayed up all night talkin' 'bout Christmas.

Joe never forgot. He did his best to raise his son right, and when Jesus went on to bigger and better things, Joe'd remember that night. When a handful of strangers helped his little family through a hard time.

He told Jesus about it when He was old enough to understand. How just a little kindness to yer fellow man can go a long way.

Jesus took it to heart.

All I Want for Christmas

By Baxter Black • Illustration By Herb Mignery

All my clothes are laundry,
   all my socks are fulla holes.
I've got t.p. in my hatband
   and cardboard in my soles.

I've stuffed the want-ad section
   underneath my long-john shirt,
And my jacket's held together
   by dehornin' blood and dirt.

The leather on my bridle's
   been fixed so many times,
My horse looks like that fence post
   where we hang the baler twine.

When I bought that horse he was
   as good as most around.
But when I sold 'im last month,
   he brought 13 cents a pound.

I've been unable lately
   to invest in purebred cows,
Since my ex-wives and their lawyers
   are dependents of mine now.

See, my first wife took my saddle,
   the second skinned my hide,
The third one got my deer head
   and the last one took my pride.

I've had a run of bad luck,
   but I think it's gonna peak,
'Cause my dog that used to bite me
   got run over just last week.

So all I want for Christmas
   is whatever you can leave,
But I'd settle for a new wife
   who would stay through New Year's Eve. 🐎

STRAYS CAUGHT IN THE GATHER

Sometimes a story just wanders onto the porch and makes himself at home.

Sometimes life is just for fun. Most of my columns, commentaries and speeches are planned to appeal to rural folks: horse people, cowboys, farmers, feed salesmen, farriers, vets, etc. It is not necessary for me to define tie-down, A-fork, gaskin, snide, pigeye, prolapse, polled, pinkeye, pendulous sheath or Pinzgauer to my regular readers.

However, on those occasions when I am addressing a more urban audience, gentiles, I call them, good folks, consumers, I become more conscious of my "cowboy vocabulary."

The stories in this final section are more generic. You don't have to be a savvy cowboy or an Arabian horse judge to enjoy them. It is part of what I call "the rubbing of cultural tectonic plates."

Granted, they are still not politically correct. In my world, blood, snot and manure are not dirty words; they are a regular part of life. I guess you could say my columns are at least biologically correct. Regarding their appropriateness, my only defense is that *Western Horseman* put them in the magazine, and that's good enough for me!

Boomer and Bernie

THERE'S BEEN A GRADUAL CHANGE in the way we cowboys do things. It's come over a period of years and coincides with anti-smoking regulations, a healthier diet, mandatory seat belts, bull riders wearing helmets, gentle horse training, improved cattle handling techniques, and not allowing our dogs free run of the pickup bed when we go to town.

It was a long time before I conceded that chaining my dog in the back was the right thing to do. It was about the time I quit speeding, chewing Copenhagen and started taking an aspirin a day. As the loss of my individual freedoms began piling up, I felt less need to let my dog enjoy one of his favorite things—riding unfettered in the back of the pickup.

Bernie, too, had faced the same decisions to do what is, begrudgingly, safer, but usually not as much fun. In his case, he lets his good cowdog Boomer ride in the front of the cab with him. Boomer liked it as long as he could have his window down far enough to hang out his head.

One fine New Mexico morning, they were driving down the Dexter highway, Bernie on the cell phone and Boomer taking in the scenery. Traffic was busy and Bernie was smack dab in the middle of a verbal therapy session with his banker. Suddenly, the cab filled with a blizzard of old receipts, magazine scraps, ear tags, Maalox pills and a roll of survey tape.

Bernie's first thought was that Boomer had hit the electric window all the way open at 45 miles an hour, but no, Boomer's body, from the neck down, was a furious flailing of limbs, scattering everything on the seat and dashboard into the air. Bernie realized immediately that Boomer had stepped on the electric window button, but he had closed it on his neck.

Bernie fought for control of the vehicle, the cell phone and the mad dog amidst the hurricane of trash that filled the air. Then, Boomer lost control of his bowels. Digested dog chow, in several stages of viscosity joined the airborne contents in the dog blender.

Swerving onto the shoulder, Bernie jumped out, raced around and jerked open the door. Boomer was still attached and smacked him on the face. As Boomer dangled momentarily, a passing motorist screamed "dog abuser!" and made an obscene gesture.

Well, Boomer got saved and Bernie now chains him in the back. He bought a gross of air fresheners to hang on the rearview mirror—they smell like cooking broccoli—and he is a changed man. Kinder and gentler, but more practical.

Yet, the profound question that lingers in his mind every time he climbs into the pickup is, "Why didn't I lower the window from the driver's side?" Maybe it was some deep man-animal bonding conflict, or perhaps simply his vision was blurred. 🐎

BAXTER
BLACK

ON THE EDGE OF COMMON SENSE

TRUTH IN LABELING

Illustration by Don Gill

WE WERE headed up a back road the other day and passed a sign that gave us pause. It read, *Intermittent Stream Ranch.*

Butch and I discussed whether possibly these folks were the victims of a new truth-in-labeling law hatched by some busybody bureaucracy. Could *Intermittent Stream Ranch* originally have been *Dry Creek Ranch?* Or even *Stuttering Brook Farms?* We began to look for other names that might fall prey to these picky-picky pontificrats.

The Mile-High City; colorful, descriptive, but certainly not completely truthful. Truth-in-labeling might require Denver to rename itself the *Somewhere-in-the-Neighborhood-of-a-Mile-High-City.*

How 'bout the *Mississippi River?* Wouldn't it be more accurate were it called the *Ten-State-Contiguous-Cooperative-Drainage-System* (and bait shop)?

Advertising a *manure spreader* might be less confusing if the advertiser distinguished between a person and a piece of machinery. Truth-in-labeling would dictate they be more specific, i.e., a *bovine night soil disseminator,* instead of a *consulting economist.*

Chicken pox: not only inaccurate, but a slam to the poultry industry as well as the Pox family in Green Forest, Arkansas. *Kid spots* is what they should be.

Freeway: At over a million dollars a mile, it should be called the *Santa Monica Expenseway.*

Does *religious right* mean they are correct all the time, and the *liberal left* mean he's gone for good?

Do the *Smoky Mountains* offer a haven for nicotine slaves?

Are the names *Garden City, New York City,* and *Des Moines* really descriptive of the towns? Would a stranger pullin' off Kansas Highway 50 through the wheat and feedlots suddenly exclaim, "This town is a garden spot! It surely must be Garden City!"?

In truth, New York is *Old York,* and I've never seen a moin in Des Moines. Why not call it *Des Corns* or *Des Pigs?*

The *Polled Hereford Digest:* Have these animals been surveyed by George Gallup? Or attacked by a group of maddened vaulters? Better the *Congenitally Unarmed Hereford Digest.*

Truth-in-labeling. Once they get started, it will never end. We'll have to change the names of the *hot dog, cowboy, gay caballero,* and *pork princess.*

Shoot, I might even have to change my name to *Frontster Caucasian, livestock husbandry person versifier.*

A congenitally unarmed Hereford.

BAXTER BLACK

ON THE EDGE OF COMMON SENSE

Why Do the Trees All Lean in Wyoming?

He said, "The wind never blows in Wyoming."
    I said, "Mister, where you from?
It'll take the top offa big R.C.
    or peel an unripened plum!

"Wherever you been, you been lied to!
    I lived in Wyoming, I know.
I once seen a horse turned clean inside out
    from standin' outside in a blow!

"You don't have to shave in the winter;
    just pick a cool, windy place.
Stand there a minute, yer whiskers'll freeze,
    and break off next to yer face!

"They claim that a boxcar in Rawlins—
    a Denver and Rio Grande—
Was picked off the tracks and blowed to the east,
    and beat the whole train to Cheyenne.

"Why, they tell of a feller in Lander
    who jumped off a bale of hay.
Before he hit ground, the wind picked 'im up—
    he came down in Casper next day!

"They don't have to shear sheep in Worland;
    when they're ready they wait for a breeze,
And bunch 'em in draws where the willers are thick,
    then pick the wool offa the trees!

"But the windiest tale that I heard
    was about the small town of Sinclair.
It used to set on the Idaho line,
    then one spring it just blew over there!

"I carry this rock in my pocket,
    for good luck and here's one for you.
Every little bit helps in Wyoming;
    if yer skinny you better take two!

"Well, stranger, you might just be part right,
    though, fer sure you ain't seen Devil's Tower.
Let's say the wind never blows in Wyoming . . .
    under 85 miles an hour!"

Illustration by
Mad Jack Hanks

"Thurlo . . . Hurry up and close that gate before the cows get out!"

Forked Limbs

AS A YOUTH, I DID THINGS that I now look back on with disbelief. There is a fine line between bravado and foolhardiness, or, as some would say, temporary insanity. We would race down gravel roads a'horseback and try to best each other by taking off each other's bridle or shirt, or loosening the cinch, all at a full gallop.

One time, Wayne's mother had made him a new pair of boxer shorts. They had hearts on them and would have fit a Percheron mule. They were so big, Wayne couldn't get them all tucked in.

Wayne, Conrad and I were loping down the berm of a big drainage ditch. I reached for Wayne and managed to grab the waistband of his new boxers just as he swung over the bank.

I stepped on the brakes and faded to the left. To his credit, he stayed in the saddle to the full extent of the elastic. I remember it as 20 or 30 feet, or at least as long as Batman's cape. Wayne spronged up like a jet pilot ejecting from his flaming F-4 Phantom!

We had another activity that was not officially approved. We called it the Tundra Leap. Leaps could be done as singles, duets or, as we once did, a triple.

Along the trail on steep-sided canyons, a rider could actually look down onto the treetops. We would stand against the backside, get a good run and dive into the top of a tree. Sometimes, we'd stand in the saddle and leap. A flip was incorporated so we would penetrate the limbs and foliage butt-first, although, depending on the thickness, one could crash through and tumble earthward.

So, when Bob told me about how he broke his ankle and scraped his face, I nodded knowingly.

He was riding a gentle 2-year-old colt named Jethro. It started to sprinkle, so Bob untied his oilskin duster and pulled it on. Just as he had both arms spread

like a preacher at the invitation, Jethro looked back.

One can only guess, but it might have appeared to him that a giant California condor was swooping down to eat him whole!

He bucked so high that Bob did a double-gainer off his back and came down in an ironwood tree, where he hung his boot in the fork of a limb six feet off the ground. (Bob is 6 feet, 2 inches.) His face lit smack in the center of a big prickly pear.

"Yeah," I said. "I know about those forked limbs." 🐎

On the Edge of Common Sense

By Baxter Black

When it's springtime in the Rockies
and my lips are turning blue
I'll be slogging through the blizzard
like a brain dead caribou. . . .

Springtime in the Rockies

Illustration by Kevin Cordtz

Ah, springtime.
That first hint of life beginning anew, the annual transformation,
its throat in long, tubercular coughs that turn rain into birdshot, sleet into ice,
Ice into snowflakes shaped like goatheads or bob wire,
not falling but slicing by you like shrapnel, sandblasting your face,
Freezing your rein hand into a claw and turning 45 degrees and balmy
into assault with intent to stupefy.

Ah, springtime.
Brave wild flowers bursting from winter's blanket, the trill of the mountain bluebird,
the exultation of a rushing brook, the whine of a spinning tire,
The splock of pliers dropped from your hand, the rattle of mudtags on a feedlot steer
that make him sound when he walks like a limping Moroccan bride.
That half brave, half scared elation of aiming your truck toward the muddy dirt road ruts
like a boat captain docking with the current, like Fast Eddy runnin' one down the rail.

Ah, springtime.
The anticipation of a new bride or a butterfly waking in his cocoon.
Like Christmas Eve with all the presents of summer waiting to be opened.
The weatherman declaring winter's over. Angels celebrating the vernal
equinox by hosing out Gabriel's hog confinement shed,
Drip drying their laundry between the mountain tops and revving up
the windchill machine for one last recalibration.

Ah, springime.
For me it's best viewed through a picture window settin' by the fire.

Once again you'll hear me promise
You'll be hearing from me soon.
When it's springtime in the Rockies
I'll be calling from Cancún. . . .

> **On the Edge of Common Sense**   BY **BAXTER BLACK, DVM**

Line Camp Tribute

KEVIN CORDTZ

DAVE IS A LOCAL RANCHER in the mountain valleys of Central California. In the spring—May 5, 2005, to be exact—he took three of his buddies into the high country to check the summer range. They four-wheeled up to the alpine zone and finally reached the line camp at Dripping Springs.

The snow-covered peaks were melting like ice cream. The spring was beautiful; the willows were budding. It was still coat-cold. Dave checked the corrals, the little outhouse, the tool shed and the spring. Then, he noticed a black bandana tied high in a birch tree that overhung the spring. He puzzled over its significance. A biker's souvenir? A hunter's signal? A cowboy's joke? A talisman? A scarecrow to drive off beavers?

He stood on his ATV and was able to reach the bandana, and managed to untie it from the limb. It seemed fresh and clean, no doubt rain and sun had laundered it well. He put it around his neck. It made him feel dashing! Inside the cabin, the larder was checked. It was kept supplied with canned goods, matches, some firewood and blankets. Notes were made on what was needed.

Dave found two cans of Miller Lite beer in the sink. "Super!" he thought, picking them up and taking them out to the spring. He set them in the icy water to cool.

The men finished the springtime cleanup, repaired a few corral poles, replenished the d-Con, nailed a shingle and repapered the outhouse.

Then, Dave dug one of the beers out of the cool spring and popped the top. Just as he was about to taunt his crew, he heard one of the boys holler from inside the cabin.

"Look at this," his friend exclaimed, holding up the guestbook that stayed in the cabin. He read aloud, "To all those who venerate the tradition of the cowboy, we, his true friends, have scattered the ashes of Charlie Blaine, one of the best buckaroos ever to work for the Dripping Springs Ranch from 1957–1971, over the spring as his final wish. May his black bandana wave until it frays and becomes part of the mountains he loved. And, instead of a statue, in his honor he asked that we leave two cans of his favorite beer as a monument to his eternal resting place."

The three men in the cabin took off their hats and paused out of respect. Dave walked in with the bandana covering his face like a bank robber and crushing the empty can.

The reader continued, "Date, May 4, 2005. May he rest in peace." 🐎

On the Edge of Common Sense

By Baxter Black

The Lone Pine

Illustration by Kevin Cordtz

"SO HOW'D yer dad git that big dent on the door?" I asked Dave.

Truth is, it was quite an accomplishment for one single dent to stand out from all the other wear and tear, deterioration, and assorted damage that covered his 1981 Ford Ranger diesel pickup truck like elephant tracks on a styrofoam cooler.

"It's a long story," sighed Dave.

Dave went with his mom and dad to gather the last of the cows off their forest permit above Feather Falls in the Sierra Madres of northern California. Dad drove the old stock truck with racks made outta airport landing strips and pulled a portable Powder River loading chute with panels. Dave followed in the Ranger.

It took 'em awhile but they finally loaded 16 head of cows and calves. Then Dad spotted one ol' cow that had held back. She'd calved recently, but the calf was nowhere in sight. They had spotted lion tracks in the vicinity. They searched till Mom, the family tracker, found the little calf under a bush.

They could feel the storm comin' and were relieved to get the last cow squeezed onto the load. They packed the loadin' chute and started down the mountain.

Dave followed in the Ranger with the new calf in the cab beside him. Bear the faithful cow dog rode in the back. Next thing he knew, Dad waved him to a stop. There was a cow down in the stock truck. Dave pulled ahead, stopped on the steep mountain road, and went back to help.

After several minutes of struggling with the down cow, Dave climbed up to say they'd need to let some of the other cows out to give her some room. It was then he noticed the Ranger, complete with dog and calf, had disappeared!

Dad was hot to catch his favorite truck when Dave pointed out that wherever it was goin', it was already there. The down cow could use some help right away.

They set up the portable chute, unloaded four cows, righted the down cow, and Dave took off to find the Ranger. He met Bear comin' back up the road at a full gallop, tail between his legs.

Around the first bend Dave could see the tip of the pickup over the side of a canyon. It had leaped off the edge and slid sideways into a lone pine. The next stop would have been 200 feet at the bottom. The calf was standin' in the seat lookin' out the back window.

Well, everybody survived although the dog won't git back in the pickup, and Dave continues to insist he left it in gear.

And Dad ... Dad still takes the hammer to the side panel now and then in an attempt to make the pine tree impression blend in with the other dents.

It's useless, though, like tryin' to make a mastodon blend in with a flotilla of mallard ducks.

On the Edge of Common Sense

By Baxter Black

Moonrise

Illustration by Don Gill

I DIDN'T HAVE time to watch the moonrise over the mountains last night. I'd gone out to get something and noticed a glow on the silhouette of China Peak. A fire, I thought. But it was still too wet for timber or brush to be burnin'.

Then, as I watched, the curve of the moon tipped over the rim. It was golden as an egg yolk and lit the sky. "How beautiful," I said to myself. It continued rising, declaring itself so fast you could almost see it moving.

I heard the horses bang the feed tub. I walked over and peeked into the corral. They gave me the eagle eye, ears up. I'd just shod the new horse and quicked his right front a little. He was standin' on it square. I felt a little lighter.

I glanced back at the moon. The top third sat on the jagged edge of the earth's incisors. It was sneakin' up on the valley.

I stared a moment. Something that big ought to be making a sound, I thought.

Like a rumbling locomotive or a creaking timber. Maybe the moaning of highline wires in a windstorm. I listened. Nothing but a night bird and the distant humming of a truck on the highway.

I found the feed tag I was looking for and stuck it in my pocket. Too late to call the feed store tonight, but I'd have it ready when I called the next morning. Then I remembered I'd promised to call the neighbor. He wanted to borrow the brush hog soon as I was done with it. I'd finished that afternoon.

I quick-stepped to the house. As I crossed the drive, I noticed the lane was dark but the tops of the trees were sparkling like they'd been sprinkled with glitter. "Man," I said to myself, "it's too bad some photographer isn't here to capture this incredible picture. No one would believe it was real."

I stepped up on the porch, made a mental note to fix the railing that was hangin' like a broken arm, and opened the screen door. I held it a moment and looked back to the east. The dogs watched me hesitate, thinkin' I might not be done outside.

The moon shone like a yellow headlight waist deep in a pool of dark water. Gonna be full tonight, I thought, as I walked to the house and made for the phone. The screen door slammed behind me and my lost opportunity.

I didn't have time to watch the moon hang itself in the sky. A scene so timeless it has been watched by Neanderthal men, pharaohs, Moses, Michelangelo, Columbus, even Pancho Villa and Garth Brooks.

But not me, I didn't have time. I had to make a call.

On the Edge of Common Sense

By Baxter Black

Clones From History

Illustration by Boots Reynolds

IF IT were possible to clone human beings from history, what would they be doing today?

For instance, if we were somehow able to find a strand of DNA from Robin Hood, clone him and raise him in our modern environment, what do you reckon he'd be doing? His genes would give him the predilection to master disguises, slink around in back rooms, and rob from the rich. Obviously, he'd be in politics.

The sheriff of Nottingham, on the other hand would rob from the rich and poor alike and have no conscience. The perfect packin' house buyer.

How 'bout Noah? Fair to middlin' navigator, knew how to make repairs en route and kept a lot of air freshener in the pilot house. He'd make a good livestock hauler.

If we cloned an Egyptian Pharaoh, where would he fit in the 20th century? Well, they spent their lifetime leaving their mark on the land for people centuries later to ponder. I believe he'd be selling Harvestore silos.

Buffalo Bill. A showman, took advantage of cowboys and stayed one jump ahead of the creditors. He could easily slip into the boots of a rodeo producer.

Edgar Allen Poe. Thought up depressing stories that scared the wits out of people. He'd be an economist.

Pancho Villa. Inspired great loyalty in his people, came from Texas, and knew all the good songs. Freddy Fender.

Attilla the Hun. Pillaged and plundered the land and built monuments to his own scorched earth policy. A real estate developer.

A Roman slave. He could own his own dairy today.

The first person who crossed the Bering Strait and introduced mastodons to the Eskimos would probably be in the llama or ostrich business now.

Lewis and Clark. Managed to make it across the country by trading trinkets to keep from getting shot. Animal health salesmen.

Chris Columbus. Had to beg for financing, made risky investments, and wound up 14,000 miles off course. He'd be feeding cattle today.

Fred Flintstone. Lived in a cave, rode a dinosaur, and didn't do well with strangers. Probably be herding sheep in Wyoming.

Nero. Played his fiddle while Rome burned. He'd probably have a BBQ joint in Branson, Missouri.

And finally Moses. He brought a plague on his neighbors, took orders from higher up, and was good with large quantities of liquid. His clone might make a good hog confinement operator. 'Course, Moses was also lost for 40 years wandering the wilderness with no apparent means of support, so he could easily be a professional team roper.

BAXTER
BLACK

ON THE EDGE OF COMMON SENSE

TOMBSTONE OF CANAAN

WANTED: A cowpoke to help gather pairs
  Dogs welcome, but not if they bark.
Non-drinker preferred, to help with the herd,
  Signed, Noah, the U.S.S. Ark.

Now Tombstone of Canaan was broke
  And, of late, had been offa the sauce,
So he rode to the yacht, was hired on the spot
  And became Noah's buckaroo boss.

"Get two of each creature on Earth."
  His orders were clear and precise.
To which he replied, "Does that include flies?
  And roaches and woolies and mice?"

He set out like he was possessed,
  He roped and delivered two skunk.
Two pigs in a poke, an egg, double yolk,
  Two elephants stuffed in a trunk.

Two jack eye, a double entendre,
  Two fish sticks still stuck to the pan
Giraffes, neck and neck, he led to the deck
  But oysters he left in the can.

He tried to get two of each specie
  A male and his counterpart
But tied in the willows were 12 armadillos
  'Cause he couldn't tell 'em apart.

He rode to the mountain and looked in the woods
  He even went downtown a'chasin'
Did the best that he could, brought 'em back on the hood,
  Two elk, two moose, and a mason.

This work had mellowed ol' Tombstone
  His heart became tender and supple.
Recanting his vow, he let in a cow
  And even a line-dancing couple.

Then Noah took Tombstone aside,
  "I'd hire you for 40 more days
If I could be sure, you'd avoid the lure
  Of the driftin' cowboy ways.

But I'm leery of takin' a cowboy,
  They just up and leave on a whim.
And though I've resisted, my arm could be twisted
  If I knew that you couldn't swim!"

Illustration by
Mike Craig

Wild Native Cowboys

MAYBE YOU'VE READ OF THE WILD ALASKAN HEREFORD HERD. They were established on an uninhabited island in the 1700s and "modernized" by ranchers in the 1960s. They are, according to their promoters, the ultimate organic beef.

"Truly 100 percent organic, receiving no growth hormones or inoculations of any kind," they say.

'Course, the freight might put them at a disadvantage, but that never stopped Perrier water or Russian caviar!

Natural selection, meaning bad winters, liver flukes, cancer eye, pneumonia, the occasional harpoon and sunburned bags, have produced a small but hearty beast, maybe like some of the herds that exist today in northern Nevada or the Gulf Coast.

I wonder if explorers will ever discover a group of wild native cowboys surviving in some uninhabited primeval forest in eastern Kentucky, or living in a bat cave near Carlsbad, New Mexico? Will they have developed physical traits suited for the life of horse and cow, like prehensile ears to reach up and pull their hats down when both hands are busy; hoof-like toenails; a large bone-spur on the back of each heel; all four fingers grown together like a spatula to lessen the chances of dally-roping injuries; large callused pads on their glutei—like a mandrill baboon—to soften the ride; or nostril flaps like a camel to keep out dust and burning hair.

The female unit would do all the bartering with nomadic groups of wild, native spear and club salesmen, and unscrupulous mammal buyers for feedlots in Nebraska. Her male counterpart, dressed in his wooly mammoth chaps and saber-tooth hatpin, would fix fence, break green Eohippi, and rope triceratopses for sport. His life span would be shorter than hers because of his tendency to do dumb things.

Natural selection has produced the ultimate organic beef up in Alaska. The process is still going on in the subspecies of wild native cowboys. No cave cowboy ever had to shoe his own Eohippus. Think of the branches of the family that were eradicated while trying to shoe horses!

Other inventions that culled out the weaker of the cowboy species were the nylon rope, the squeeze chute, the metal gate and the fence staple.

Now, here we are, living in a new century and holding our hands in front of our faces, daring anybody, "Betcha can't hit my hand before I move it!" 🐎

On the Edge of Common Sense

By Baxter Black

Old Ways Die Hard

Illustration by
Kevin Cordtz

OLD WAYS die hard. Even after Gary converted his western Nebraska cow operation to four-wheelers, Ambro still thought of the mechanical monster as his horse.

"I broke the horse," Ambrosia said in his melodious Spanish accent. Gary had found him waiting at the little office when he came to work at 6:30 a.m. Ambro had always said "he don't want the sun to get too heavy" on him, so he started early.

"You broke the horse?" asked Gary, ready for anything. "What do you mean?"

According to Ambro, he had been out sorting cow-calf pairs that morning. One big calf kept ducking under the 3-strand barbwire fence. Frustrated, Ambro took his "horse'" through the wire gate to git the calf back. He had been a *bueno vaquero* in his youth and prided himself on his roping. He tied hard and fast to the mechanical saddle horn and took up the chase.

The handlebar clutch, throttle and brake "reins" made swinging his loop and car-

rying his coils a little unwieldy. The calf was quick and led Ambro around the flat and through the swales like dry leaves being chased by a lawn mower.

In the clattering banging commotion Ambro dropped a coil, maybe two, around a front tire, which promptly tightened against the knot tied to the handlebar saddle horn, which jerked the "horse" to a stop.

Ambro dismounted, got enough slack in the line to peel the rope off the wheel horse's foot. It took off … by itself! Being still in third high, the chase gear, it began making circles around the vaquero, who held tight to the other end of the rope like a longe line. All he needed was a whip to complete the training picture.

"I tink," he had explained to Gary, "I should let go … what could happen?" He did; his "horse" disappeared over a hump in the direction of the cows, going home like all good horses do.

Ambro chased it but it could run faster. He topped the rise and surveyed the scene below. "I don't know, Boss, but it hit the fence, turn sideways under the wire, and run along below. It was liftin' up the wire and tearin' out the T-posts till it hit the wooden railroad tie. It was bouncing up and down on its hind legs like Trigger tryin' to jump it. I went up to him real easy and said 'whoa' and switch the key. But it was too late … my horse was broke."

Gary was pounding his desk and snorting like a Percheron. Tears were streaming down his face. He was gasping.

Ambro was confused. In his polite old country way, he said, "I wanted to laugh, too, but … I had to catch my breath first." 🐎

ON THE EDGE OF COMMON SENSE | BY BAXTER BLACK

Ay, Chihuahua!

We crossed the border at Antelope Wells, New Mexico, 40 miles south of Hachita on Highway 81, which is paved right up till your front tire hits Mexico. It must be the loneliest immigration outpost in the country. We drove 72 miles from Animas, New Mexico, to Mexico Highway 2, in the middle of the day and passed only one car that wasn't up on blocks. The U.S. agent held us for 10 minutes just to visit. We agreed to write him occasionally, and he finally let us through. We didn't wake the Mexican border guard.

It's big country in northern Chihuahua, big and brown. They're in a years-long drought. Cow numbers steadily declined as ranchers sold off. No grass, no feed. What's left are down to eating prickly pear and bird nests.

We arrived at our destination, a big ranch, northwest of Janos — 50,000 acres, a 40-kilometer driveway, its own chapel, its own mountain range, its own pen of goats. The big rancho, where we spent the next two days, looked like a Hollywood movie set. A beautiful rock hacienda with a courtyard was surrounded by freshly painted cottages for the help, a large cookhouse and a quaint white stucco Catholic chapel complete with cross and bell.

The hacienda's indoor décor was elaborate and rich, befitting the now-incarcerated drug lord who'd been the previous owner. The silent presence of malathion was appreciated in the obvious absence of roaches, scorpions and centipedes. I was accompanying Dr. Harold, a U.S. Department of Agriculture veterinarian who monitors the spaying of Mexican heifers for import to the United States. Sexually complete, fertile cattle must undergo lengthy testing for brucellosis and tuberculosis

at the border. Spaying the females shortens the delay considerably.

The facilities were good. Two Mexican veterinarians did the surgery. Two squeeze chutes ran simultaneously, and two ovaries were laid on each heifer's back as proof — 505 heifers in 5 ½ hours, one every 46 seconds, cost to rancher $8 to $12 (U.S.) per heifer. The spayed heifers were given an official U.S. Food and Drug Administration ear-tag, and they were branded with an MX on the right hip. I felt a renewed respect for our government veterinary corps.

We ate all meals in the cookhouse with the cowboys. Beans and tortillas every meal, with a different spicy side-meat each time. I didn't keep track of the chickens

and goats in the yard, but the large parrot in the courtyard that greeted our arrival was missing when we left.

The trip home included a pass through a Mennonite community, where you could buy a soda pop for 50 cents, 2 ½ pounds of homemade cheese for $3.50 and gas for $2 per gallon.

Chihuahua was another world, and yet punchin' cows through a chute, visitin' with cow people and bein' able to see the stars at night was no different than if I was in Oregon, Kansas or Georgia.

I felt right at home. 🐎

On the Edge of Common Sense

By Baxter Black

Duct Tape in Agriculture

Illustration by Don Gill

A collection of testimonials . . .

From B.A., large animal vet:

I've been a duct tape believer ever since I had a cow tear her bag on a bob-wire fence. It was a ghastly gash. She was in pain and frightened. There was no way I could close the wound until . . . I began wrapping her with duct tape! I started just behind the elbow and started circling her girth, then her ribs and her flanks with duct tape. I eventually was able to wrap the bag, leaving the four teats and tail poking out. Six months later the tape fell off and she was cured!

From F.W., horseshoer:

One afternoon I had been called to shoe a miniature horse. I was expecting one in the St. Bernard-Great Dane class, but this one was not much bigger than a medium house cat. I built to the task and was bent over the left hind leg when my nipper slipped. I had accidentally trimmed the hoof clear off the hock. I panicked until . . . I remembered the roll of duct tape I always keep in my watch pocket. Using 4-inch bolts, I splinted the leg back together and wrapped it with duct tape. Two months later it seems to be working, although he's still walking funny.

From D.W., poultry pathologist:

Doing surgery on chickens is uncommon. Whenever I saw a chicken he was usually dead. And yet many suffered from ingrown feathers. Most *polloqueros* (chicken cowboys from Mexico) spent hours each day gently plucking the ingrown feathers from afflicted hens. One afternoon I was helping and happened to drop a chicken on a strip of duct tape I had circled around my feet to stave off fire ants. When I picked up the chicken her brisket was plucked clean. Inspired, the polloqueros completely wrapped me with duct tape, sticky side out, and slapped the chicken's afflicted area containing the ingrown feather against my body. This technique has since been adopted to declaw cats and in beauty shops as a depilatory.

From Y.K., team roper:

I used to carry rawhide, latigo, hole punchers, awls, Chicago screws, harness buckles, rubber wraps, bell boots, Super Glue, baby powder, rivets, snaps, curb chains, and fencing pliers in my emergency box. Now all I carry is duct tape. I've used it to repair broken cinches, lengthen reins, rebuild hondas, plait manes, wrap horns, tie on, dress wounds, plug bloody noses, and replace thumbs. I now wear chinks made out of duct tape, have padded my saddle with duct tape, and braided a nice hat band with duct tape.

Today I have covered my pickup with duct tape and written "Born to Rope" in duct tape on the side of my trailer. I'm ready and lookin' for a header. Just call 1-800-DuckTap.

BAXTER BLACK

ON THE EDGE OF COMMON SENSE

Rich Farming

Illustration by Kevin Cordtz

If wheat gets up to seven bucks
   I'll hoard it, yessiree
Till the grain bin's overflowin'
   or it gets back down to three

There's too much ridin' on it
   to sell it right away
The banker might call in my note
   they're funny that-a-way

As long as things are nip and tuck
   they'll let the balance ride
Just pay the interest on it
   and they'll be satisfied

They don't like sudden changes
   conservatives, you see
They like things they can count on
   like hail and CRP

And if you look to go prosperous
   or friends think that you are
They'll try and sell you somethin'
   you've lived without, so far

Like asphalt on the driveway
   or fancy silverware
Or a double-jointed tractor
   course, the preacher wants his share

No, there ain't no use me gettin' rich
   knowin' me, I'd spend it
And borrow more for land and stock
   there's plenty who would lend it

I'm better off just gettin' by
   and stayin' where I set
'Cause the more I make farmin'
   the more I go in debt

So, if wheat goes up to seven
   I could sell it on the board
But I won't, 'cause makin' money's
   one thing I can't afford

It's a different kind of logic
   that allows a man to boast
When the richest farmer farmin'
   is the one who owes the most

On the edge of common sense

By Baxter Black

Salesman's dilemma

I HAD sold a magic bolus to a farmer.
It was guaranteed to rid his herd of flies.
It would pass out with the pucky
And if everyone got lucky
It would kill the eggs the flies laid in the pies.

He had bought enough to do a hundred critters.
"These had better work," he said, "they cost enough."
"I can guarantee they'll do it,
I'll come out and take you through it—
You just follow the directions for the stuff."

Illustration by Kevin Cordtz

I drove out and found the farmer nearly finished.
But the scene I saw sent shivers up my spine.
Was the A.I. tech invited?
Had the farmer grown near-sighted?
'Cause a crowd had gathered 'round the cow's behind.

In the middle wearin' goggles and a slicker
Smeared with green effluent like he'd hit the fan,
Dressed in precomposted splendor,
Poised at the ready to rear-end her,
Stood the farmer with a balling gun in hand.

"How's it goin', boys?" I asked with trepidation.
"Well, this bothers some cows more than I'd 'uve thought.
This procedure don't impress her."
I said, *"Try a tongue depressor."*
But I knew that all his work had been for naught.

So I watched him put the bolus … I can't say it.
My commission check was goin' up in smoke.
I was gonna take a skinnin'
Then I saw the whole crew grinnin'
And I realized they'd staged it as a joke!

At the office when I told my boss the story
He got livid, said I'd bollixed up the sale.
"Now we'll have to go redo 'em,
What the heck did you say to 'em?"
"Nuthin'. Since they only had ten left … I held the tail."

On the Edge of Common Sense

By Baxter Black

Two-Man Jobs

Illustration by
J.P. Rankin

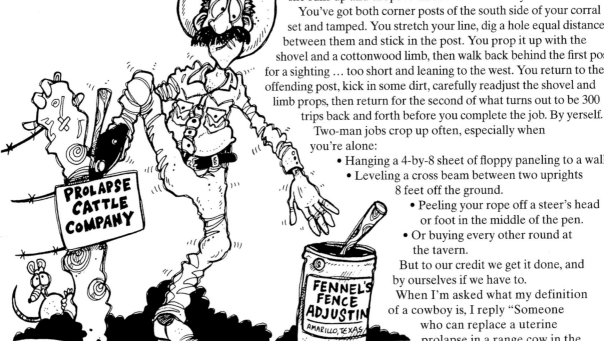

SO THERE I was pulling one end of the wire, patching fence. The strand lay stretched tight in the claw of the hammer which I had balanced against the post, bracing it with my leg. I sighted down the wire, peeking under my arm, and raised the wire half an inch … perfect. I took the staple from my lips and set it against the post just behind the barb and reached for my pounding hammer, which lay exactly 3 inches beyond my grasp. Attempting to barb it, I imitated a contortionist trying to bite off his toenail, all to no avail.

I turned to my assistant … Are you kidding! I had no assistant. Just another case of one man doin' a two-man job.

You run the cow down the alley nearly into the squeeze chute, manage to cram a piece of pipe behind her, run around the chute, open the head gate wide to entice her to come forward, close the tailgate, keeping one hand on the head lever you try and kick her through the bars as she sulls up and drops to all fours. I turn to my assistant …

You've got both corner posts of the south side of your corral set and tamped. You stretch your line, dig a hole equal distance between them and stick in the post. You prop it up with the shovel and a cottonwood limb, then walk back behind the first post for a sighting … too short and leaning to the west. You return to the offending post, kick in some dirt, carefully readjust the shovel and limb props, then return for the second of what turns out to be 300 trips back and forth before you complete the job. By yerself.

Two-man jobs crop up often, especially when you're alone:

• Hanging a 4-by-8 sheet of floppy paneling to a wall.
• Leveling a cross beam between two uprights 8 feet off the ground.
• Peeling your rope off a steer's head or foot in the middle of the pen.
• Or buying every other round at the tavern.

But to our credit we get it done, and by ourselves if we have to.

When I'm asked what my definition of a cowboy is, I reply "Someone who can replace a uterine prolapse in a range cow in the middle of a 3-section pasture with nothing but a rope and a horse."

We who work the land are that wonderful combination of cleverness, belligerence and immunity to pain. 🐎

ON THE EDGE OF COMMON SENSE | BY BAXTER BLACK

Cow Painting

My wife collects cow art. I don't think it was anything she planned, or if it was even her idea. She once worked for the state cattle-growers association and always has had an "Eat Beef" license on the front of her car. So, I suspect somebody gave her a small cow knick-knack.

Later, a neighbor was visiting, saw the knick-knack and concluded she collected cows. When the occasion arose for a gift, the same neighbor gave my wife another cow knick-knack. An avalanche began. Now our house is festooned with photos, paintings, statuettes, refrigerator magnets, key chains, temp tats, sweaters, sweatshirts and hoof-and-horn motif.

When cities began displaying life-sized, painted plastic cows on street corners and in store windows, the barrage increased. I've never quite understood the painted cow (or horse, buffalo or wombat) art, though it's very creative. A piano company, for instance, displayed a grand cow with her rib cage propped open and a keyboard for teeth. A jeweler had a water-belly steer covered with glistening calculi stones, and a Mexican food restaurant's cow would look like a piñata.

But where did the idea come from? I think I know. The story has been passed down through the generations of Sierra Nevada ranchers, California vaqueros and sale-barn bull-haulers until it's achieved legend proportions.

Señor Geraldo, rich rancher, good neighbor and Angus man, noticed one of his bulls was gone. He called his neighbor, another wealthy landlord and cattle baron.

Sure enough, Geraldo's bull was running rampant in the neighbor's pen of crossbred heifers. Señor Geraldo saddled his registered purebred, standing-at-stud stallion, loaded and trailered him to the neighbors, sorted off the bull and, with much whacking and colorful drover language, trailered him home.

The next morning the bull had escaped and returned to the neighbor's fertile playground. Geraldo repeated the saddling, loading, whacking and cursing, but the bull stood his ground. Help was called.

A local cowboy saddled, loaded and drove to lend assistance. Alas, even two *buen* caballeros couldn't move the stubborn bull.

Geraldo returned home dejected. Riding in, he noticed his three sons, Princes One, Two and Three, practicing with their paint-ball guns. An idea formed. He loaded the young princes and their armory into the old ranch truck and returned to the neighbors. With the windows rolled down and boys sticking out like queens on a parade float, he drove up behind the bull and ordered, "Open fire!" They fired, circled, reloaded, fired, circled constantly moving closer to the corral gate until the bull finally tucked his tail and retreated.

The truck, both inside and out, was thoroughly painted, as were the pistoleros, half the cows, the back of Geraldo's hat, and one side-mirror that now hung like a broken arm. But at least half of the paint balls had struck their target. The bull looked like a stained-glass window. Had it not been for his pendulous sheath and a white spot on his belly, you wouldn't have known he was an Angus.

And this began the ancient tradition of painting urban cows. Honest. No bull. 🐎

On the Edge of Common Sense

By Baxter Black

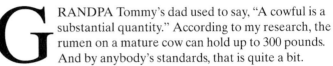

A Cowful

Illustration by Mike Craig

GRANDPA Tommy's dad used to say, "A cowful is a substantial quantity." According to my research, the rumen on a mature cow can hold up to 300 pounds. And by anybody's standards, that is quite a bit.

Say you had a cowful of pocket change. You'd almost need a cow to keep it in. Say you had a cowful of wet laundry. It would take a forklift to get it in the dryer. Say you had a cowful of manure.

Well, I guess a lot of us do.

If cowful became an accepted unit of measure, it could replace the antiquated English standards like the dram and the rod. And those bland, simple-minded metric names that somehow sound communistic: kiloliter, hectometer, decigram. Can you picture in your mind a decigram? Is it the weight of a decimated graham cracker? Or 10 grandmas standin' on the scale?

Under the cowful system, 15 scoopfuls would equal a cowful.

Two bootfuls would make a scoopful; 2 hatfuls would make a bootful. Half a hatful would equal a capful.

Six canfuls, as in beer cans, makes a capful. One canful equals 40 thimblefuls; 20 teardrops in a thimbleful.

The dosage for penicillin would read: 4 teardrops per 5 scoopfuls of body weight IM.

For blackleg four-way vacination: 1 thimbleful SQ. Repeat in 60 days.

Bizarre, you say. If cowful was a measure of weight or volume, possibly the distance between postholes would become the standard unit of measure for length; for example, 660 postholes per section line, 4 thumbs to a hand, 3 hands to a foot, 4 feet to a coyote length, and 2 coyote lengths to a posthole.

Decibels of loudness would be described in more understandable terms, from chicken peck to pig squeal for everyday sounds. Loud noises would be categorized as small wreck, big wreck, and heck'uva wreck.

"So, did you hear about Orbin gettin' bucked off? Musta sailed 5 coyote lengths, hit the side of the grain bin with a moose bugle, and 2 cowfuls of pellets fell on him. Smashed him flatter'n a rabbit ear.

"They got him to the Doc in half a coon's age, transfused him with a six-pack of type-O negative, and removed a posthole of intestine. He's doin' okay, but he's lost about 6 hatfuls.

"He's been a sheep's gestation recovering. Doc says it's shock, but I figger it just scared a pea waddin' and a half out of him. Well, I gotta go. I've got an appointment in 4½ shakes of a lamb's tail."

On the Edge of Common Sense

By Baxter Black

The Cowboy Vegetarian Cookbook

When beef gets short, a lot of cowboys are forced to do without. The cook must come up with meatless meals. The following recipes are from the Cowboy Vegetarian Cookbook.

Tennis Shoe Tongue: Select an old one. The price is better and it may have picked up some natural flavor depending on where it has been worn. Boiling is suggested but it may also be fried to a crisp and served on a hot bed of marinated sweat shirt. Garnish with pickled shoe string.

Seed Corn Cap Pizza: Carefully clean with a fish scaling knife. Remove all metal buttons, rivets, and any plastic tabs. Flatten the cap by soaking in linseed oil then placing it under a door mat that gets heavy use. Once pliable, cover it with lots of cheese and ketchup. Dry kibbles or dust motes may be sprinkled as a topping for variety.

Meadow Hay Salad: Choose a bale toward the middle of the stack. Break the bale, being careful to remove any plastic twine. Take a flake and winnow it over the garage floor. Then chop the stems with a heavy blunt utensil like a bucket or hoe. For dressing, pound a kumquat-sized piece of 17 percent protein block on a flat surface and add vinegar. Croutons chipped from corn cobs or diced styrofoam may be tossed in. Feed whatever is left to the cows.

Fan Belt Fajitas: The most succulent fan belt can be found on old farm equipment moldering in your boneyard. It should be sliced into bite-sized chunks. Tenderize before cooking by soaking in fingernail polish remover. Fry in lard along with half a hatful of ¾-inch black plastic hose and shredded playing cards. Serve with beer and jalapenos. It tastes a lot like abalone.

Rawhide Stew: Ever wondered what to do with those old reins, quirts, or saddle tree bark? This recipe has been tried and tested from ancient Mongolians right up through Donner Pass. Place the strips of rawhide in a pot and boil for as many weeks as firewood holds out. What you add to the stew depends on what's available: for example, pine cones, hoof trimmings, iron pyrite, or old hat brims. It's filling but don't expect much more.

Roasted Kak: Ever eat a saddle? Some parts are edible. Dig a hole big enough to bury a small mule. Burn elm, cottonwood, and old tires to get a bed of coals. Wrap the saddle in a plastic tarp (blue), place it on the coals, and cover with dirt. Cook for hours on end. Dig up and serve with baked faucet washers. Feeds up to two truckloads of hungry cowboys.

That should give you an idea of what you can do when you run out of beef at the ranch. There are many other Cowboy Vegetarian recipes like Latigo Jerky, Gunstock Pate, and Smokin' Joe's Copenhagen Torte, but this should get you started. 🐎

Illustration by Don Gill

❯ On the Edge of Common Sense

BY **BAXTER BLACK, DVM**

Hat Tricks

WHEN I'M IN AN AIRPORT, I always wave at a cowboy hat … a real cowboy hat. Somehow, you can spot 'em. They inevitably turn out to be some bull rider on the way to a rodeo, a state cattlemen's association representative on the way to Washington, D.C., or a consultant of some kind, or farmer or rancher on the way to a funeral or a graduation.

Hats take a pretty good beating in the overhead storage on the airplanes. I got off the plane in Southern Colorado, grabbed my hat from above— and it had been smashed by a suitcase. My hat looked like it had been rained on, then put in a lunchbox to dry!

I drove into town, found a Western store and asked if I could borrow their steamer. "Of course," they said. "Have at it."

Junior ambled over to visit. He occupied the job of "old-timer" in the store. He looked at my hat and asked if I'd backed over it with a D-8 Cat.

It reminded him of one time when he and his pardner were out lookin' for some cows. It was high up in the fall, and they were makin' the last round for stragglers. Between them they had 17 horses, and when they needed to change, they'd just go in the corral and rope one. He said they didn't always catch the ones they were aiming for.

Like that day. He caught one that had the tendency to erupt on occasion. It coincided with the day he wore his new hat. The horses were sharp-shod with screws in the horseshoes, like caulks, to better navigate the treacherous ice. Sure 'nuf, on a downhill grade Spook came apart and bucked Junior over his head. Junior's hat flew off, and Spook came down with two steel front paws right in the middle of his new felt hat.

That punched so many holes in it, he said, after that when he wore it in the wind, he sounded like a piccolo.

Another time, he was pushing cows along the edge of the Dolores River, riding a kid horse. Suddenly, the cows broke and ran! The ol' pony was steady, and they rode on up to see what scared the cows: a bear maybe, mountain lion, who knew? They broke through the willows to a little clearing and were confronted by two river travelers—campers maybe—women coming right toward them, wearing … sunglasses, that's all, just sunglasses! They screamed! Junior screamed! The kid pony reared up, rolled back and evacuated the area! Junior lost his hat.

He went back for it, but had to walk the last 50 feet; kid pony wouldn't go any farther. Oh, and he never found his hat.

Maybe the Nashville, Santa Fe, Aspen, Toby Keith kind of floppy, dishrag hat, which looks like a regurgitated hippopotamus cud, does have some practical value after all. It comes pre-smashed— perfect for the cowboy frequent flyer. 🐎

ON THE EDGE OF COMMON SENSE | BY BAXTER BLACK

Out There

ILLUSTRATION BY KEVIN CORDTZ

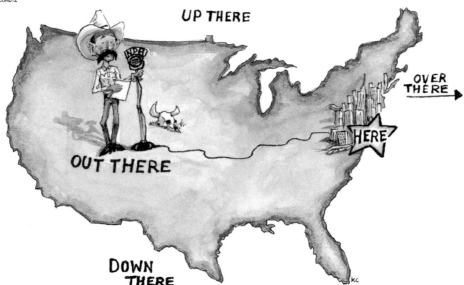

I do commentary on National Public Radio headquartered in Washington D.C. It's heavily urban in listenership. Some have questioned why NPR includes my commentaries. So have I. When I asked, the producer said, "Because you're the only one we know … from *out there*."

Out there. Where exactly is … out there? When I look south from my veranda I can see as far back in time as Coronado, who rode up the river horseback and came within 5 miles of my house. That was in 1535, 300 years before those johnny-come-latelys Lewis and Clark caught a ride with the locals to Fort Pierre.

When I look toward the north on a crystal clear night, I can see as far away as Polaris, axle of the Big Dipper. It shines directly down on the outposts of civilization. Omak, Sandpoint, Viking, Culbertson, Maple Creek, Elgin, Eagle Butte and Newcastle. Settlements as self-sufficient and self-reliant as a space station on the surface of the moon. Places where people and elm trees send down roots and look with pity at those who have to send out for pizza at 10 til seven because they don't have their act together.

When I look to the sunrise I can see clear back to the palmetto and piney woods, Cumberland Gaps and cornfields. Where many of the gringo ancestors walked and rode, and intermarried and populated the Llano Estacado, the arid plains, the holes in the walls and the ends of the roads. Like the boll weevil, lookin' for a home.

When I look to the setting sun, I hear the jingle of the bit chains, the swish of the lariat, the beat of the drum, and war cry of the natives and Spaniards who named the places we live, Maricopa, Kaibab, Santa Rosa, Tonapah, Tillamook, Durango and Winnemucca, and still live there.

When I look down, I see the paw print of a mountain lion in a sandy wash, the outline of a steel shoe that I nailed to my horse's foot, a black porous rock that was belched up from earth's inferno before people walked here. And the track of my son who passed this way this morning to do the chores.

And when I look up I hear the silence, the rustle of things jostling for position in space. The cry of the coyote and the heavenly admonition to use the place responsibly, to appreciate its harsh beauty and to pick up the trash.

Out there. A vast part of this country from the Sierras to the backwoods, north and south as far as you can point, where the tracks are further apart, and you can see the stars at night.

Out there. No better, no worse, just a little leaner and closer to the bone.

When the NPR producer had said, "Because you're the only one from out there," I wondered if he meant geographically or philosophically?

I'm still not sure. 🐎

ON THE EDGE OF COMMON SENSE | BY BAXTER BLACK

Palmetto

I remember the first time I ever went to Florida. It was in the cow country around Wauchula that I first saw palmetto. Copses of palm trees, cypress and yellow pine stood like islands in a sea of green grass. Hammocks, the locals called the "islands," were carpeted with low-lying, exotic-looking, jagged-leafed plants. From a distance it appeared to be professionally landscaped. "Palmetto," they said.

I was reminded of that day last winter, when a visitor stared out on a flat Arizona desert pasture packed paddle to paddle, joint to joint with prickly pear and cholla. He remarked that it looked like a xeriscaped garden feature in *Arizona Highways*. But, as any cow, cowboy or horse can tell you, a chase through a cholla forest is akin to being attacked by an army of maddened kindergarten teachers armed with staple guns!

I learned later, after chasing a cow through the palmetto, that it, too, isn't as innocent as brushing up against a feather boa. It grows in giant clumps of tangley roots and stems. Rough and hard as cottonwood bark, big as small culverts with stiff, sharp, spiny, saw-toothed leaves. Riding through it can be compared to tiptoeing through a bed of petrified sewer pipe all wrapped in porcupine coats.

Palmettos are very difficult plants to eradicate, my friend Henry confirmed. In an effort to improve the value of his house in town, Henry decided that a lawn in back would be a nice place to entertain friends. Certainly, when compared to its present moonscape/landfill motif that featured ragweed, a dead plum tree sapling and the engine block off his '73 Dodge pickup.

His county agent suggested an initial fertilizing and rototilling. Thrifty Henry made arrangements with the local feedlot to simply wash out three livestock trailers in his backyard. The deed was done. Three loads of 200-weight 3-year-olds from the Everglades were unloaded at the feedlot, and the trailers hosed out in Henry's yard. Apparently the calves had been eating palmetto seeds.

By June, Henry's yard looked like a pineapple field. By July, a tequila plantation, in August a green oil refinery! Henry fought back with Weedeaters, tin snips, machetes, chainsaws, Spanish goats, backhoes, spray planes, dynamite and nuclear weapons. For three years he tried to beat back the green tsunami that threatened to overtake his home. Finally he sold it to a snowbird from Chicago, who covered the whole backyard with a net and built a parrot sanctuary.

In our innocence we see beauty in the world around us. Just last week a lady in town remarked on the beauty of the tall purple-plumed plants blooming in the bar ditch on the way to town. Russian thistle, I explained. 🐴

KEVIN CORDTZ

ON THE EDGE OF COMMON SENSE | BY BAXTER BLACK

The Great Trailer Purchase

ILLUSTRATION BY KEVIN CORDTZ

It finally happened. The leaf-spring broke, the fender peeled the tread off the left rear tire and the Valdez gave up the ghost. My 1972, 16-foot, bumper-pull Hale stock trailer, so named because of the spillage it left in its wake whilst loaded to the scuppers with juicy cows.

I contacted the Mecca of stock trailers, Madill, Okla. They sent brochures from trailer manufacturers, information on coon dogs and pamphlets from the Southern Baptist Church. I bought a new 16-foot gooseneck over the phone and asked my son-in-law if he could deliver it. He agreed, loaded it with 90 bales of grass hay for which he'd paid $1.75 each, and came west. On arrival I offered him $3 per bale, he sold it for $5.50 and I paid his diesel and per diem.

Gerald liked my new trailer. We discussed how he could take advantage of a similar delivery scheme. I warned him, though the price was right, it was a pretty lightweight trailer. He'd been

pullin' a 24-foot gooseneck that Lewis and Clark used on their first trip west that weighed as much empty as it did loaded. But you could jump 10 horses in it and still have room to park a Kubota in back. But it was more than he needed.

A 10-foot gooseneck was what he thought he'd like. My question was, "Why?" He had no sheep. Never mind. He found it, a 1980 barely used dual-axle, custom-shortened, 10-foot gooseneck stock trailer, reinforced steel, mint condition that had been up on blocks for 6 years.

He offered the widow $2,500. "Is that what it's worth?" she asked innocently. "That's what it's worth to me," he replied.

Gerald wrote her a check and pulled it off.

I could tell he was proud of his purchase, as he gave me a walking tour of the trailer. It was beautiful. I remarked he sure got a good deal on it. But I couldn't imagine there was much of a buyers' market for a 10-foot gooseneck. It's like

Kenworth shocks on a riding mower. The widow's son even called Gerald, asking if the price had been fair.

It reminded me of my best lifetime purchase. A 1969 F-250 pickup, four-speed, camper special, in mint condition, 20 years old, 42,000 miles, complete with camper. It, too, had belonged to a widow. She priced the gem herself and I jumped at the deal. I sold the camper for $500 and I'm still drivin' the truck.

Gerald and I mulled over these good deals, justifying our purchases and convincing each other that it was fair to all concerned. But it did cross my mind, what if Gerald and I happened to reach the pearly gates at the same time? Saint Peter might give us the eagle eye and ask, "Aren't you the two cowboys that took advantage of those sweet old ladies? As penance we're gonna let you work in the heavenly tire department ... fixin' split rims and rewiring old trailers for the first thousand years. Next." 🐎

ON THE EDGE OF COMMON SENSE | BY BAXTER BLACK

Helicopters and Dirigibles

I get mail from men and women stationed in Iraq and Afghanistan. They're mostly from cowboys serving in uniform, and so inevitably "wrecks" happen that only a cowboy could appreciate.

The military is using reconnaissance dirigibles, balloons lighter than air, to detect enemy presence and to protect bases from terrorist activities. They're tethered to the ground by a cable and go hundreds of feet in the air, not unlike Napoleon used 200 years ago during some of his battles. Although Napoleon had a Frenchman in a basket with binoculars, the modern dirigibles are unmanned, filled with the latest photographic and digital surveillance devices available, and monitored by a ground crew.

KEVIN CORDTZ

Out of the clear blue of the Persian sky, a helicopter approached the base, and one of its blades hit a dirigible cable! A quick call was made to headquarters as they watched the freed balloon rising into the prevailing winds and drifting toward Iran.

I'm sure many of you cowboys at home are thinking, "What would I do?" A biplane with a hook, or a team roper on the wing? A helicopter approach from the top, lowering a bull rider onto the dirigible with his Moore Maker balloon-piercing knife? Have two fly fishermen from Bozeman parachute by and reel it in?

Not the Air Force. They called in an F-15 Eagle with instructions to intercept and disable the dirigible gingerly so the billion dollars' worth of top-secret equipment could be recovered. Explicit instructions over the radio ordered, "Be careful not to hit the instrument cluster."

"Roger, Captain!"

On the initial, and only, strafing pass, the deadeye pilot pulled down on the target and pressed the trigger. The explosion could be heard at the Syrian Embassy in Fort Worth, Texas!

Al Jazeera's heart skipped a beat! It lit up the sky like a sunrise! Flaming clumps, shreds and pieces cleaved the atmosphere like streaking meteorites into the wild blue yonder! It was obliterated, all save one piece of twisted scrap metal about the size of a Volkswagen that was found 10 miles away.

I understand the pilot is in the process of applying for a medal recognizing his valor in recovering and disabling top-secret material before it fell into enemy hands.

The hunk has been recycled and is now a doorstop in the mess tent.

On the Edge of Common Sense

By Baxter Black

Visiting Dogs

Illustration by
J.P. Rankin

WHEN I hear a truck pull up in front of the house and the pandemonium of dogs barkin' would wake a hibernating mastodon, I relax. It's only my neighbor, D.K., come to borrow something of his back.

He doesn't get this ferocious reception because he's on the canine list of unsavory visitors or because he has the reputation of annoying domestic animals on a regular basis. It's because his two dogs usually accompany him on his rounds.

My dogs even bark at his pickup when he drives in anticipation that his dogs will be in the back. On those rare occasions when he comes "undogged," my dogs give him a withering stare and stomp off. It's like they are disappointed.

After all, what else have they got to do? Watch the sheep through the fence? Go to the pasture and check the cows? Sneak up on the creek in hopes of scaring the urea out of the ducks? Go roll in the dead carp stranded on the bank?

I watched them the last time I went to D.K.'s to borrow his brush hog. My dogs were leaning out the side, already clearing their throats as we neared his place. I deliberately drove by the first turn-in. Both dogs jerked their heads around and glared at me through the back window. I could see Hattie mouthing the words, "Hey, Turkey, ya missed it!"

I turned in the second drive and we were met with the raucous sounds of a rabbit let go in a dog kennel. I pulled to a stop as D.K.'s dogs surrounded the pickup, barking at the top of their dog lungs.

My dogs were leaning out over the side like seasick fishermen returning in kind, bark for bark. It was deafening.

But I noticed D.K.'s dogs never got quite close enough to touch noses, and mine knew just how far to lean to avoid actual contact.

One might think it was all for show. Protecting their territory, as if his were shouting, "Don't you dare get out," and mine were screaming, "No way we're letting you jump in this truck!"

Or they could just be visiting like old folks at a reunion:

"HOW ARE YOU TEX! I HEAR YOU GOT A NEW HEARING AID! WHAT KIND IS IT?"

"QUARTER TO FOUR!"

I've gotten to where I don't worry about it much. Dogs like to bark. It's in their job description. It probably doesn't irritate the dogs near as much as it does us humans. They just communicate at different decibel levels. It's part of nature. It's possible even aphids bark at each other, and we just can't hear it.

But it must drive the ants crazy.

JP RANKIN © 2000
"THE CARTOON COWBOY"

BIG DOG RANCH

ON THE EDGE OF COMMON SENSE | BY BAXTER BLACK

Learning by Hand

There are some things you can learn only by hand. Imagine reading a book with instructions on how to milk a cow, i.e.,

1. Secure the beast.
2. Grasp the teat.
3. Squeeze and pull.

The same instructions (with slight alterations) could apply to picking an orange, lancing a boil, cracking a safe or trying to open one of those titanium-formed plastic wraps that a new tool or toy comes in.

The cow-milking instructions skip the parts about a scoop of grain, loose head catch, cow kicks, letdown, flies, switches with cockleburs, flying manure and the carbs in strawberry-flavored tit dip!

I think of the knowledge required when I send my son to the next ridge, to check for cows on the other side. Although I've spent hours on end explaining things to him,

words alone can't give him a feel for his horse, a sense of where to cross an arroyo, an ability to spot a cow amid her mesquite camouflage, a caution of "snaky" places and the increasing confidence that takes him farther from me every day.

He continues to increase his cowboy savvy with every ride, every gather and every branding. Every morning when he feeds the horses, the dogs and the birds, he adds sediment to his sea of knowledge. Knowledge accrued by hand.

There are subjects that can be taught in a classroom, such as history, pharmacology, social studies or political science, topics a student might grasp without "lifting a finger," so to speak. But as soon as you

drift into chemistry, computer science or agronomy, you're forced to participate more than cerebrally to learn the subject. Thus chemistry lab, soil judging and mouse training.

Is it possible to be a piano teacher and not be able to play the piano? Theoretically, maybe. But most useful skills require a hands-on approach. Children progress from learning how to shovel with a spoon, to whistling, to making that obnoxious sound by placing their hands under their armpits and pumping.

So, while there might be millions of books written about how to improve your golf game, train your horse or flatten your abs, unless you put that knowledge into practice you'll never truly learn how. And practice you must; here, let me get my hand inside my shirt and show you. 🐎

On The Edge Of Common Sense

By Baxter Black, D.V.M.

In Defense of the Chicken

Illustration by Robert M. Miller, D.V.M.

Everybody says they love chicken,
   Ambrosia sent from above.
But nobody loves a chicken,
   A chicken ain't easy to love.

It's hard to housebreak a chicken,
   They just don't make very good pets.
You might teach one bird imitations
   But that's 'bout as good as it gets.

Mentally, they're plumb light-headed
   And never confused by the facts.
That's why there's no seein' eye chickens,
   Guard chickens, or trained chicken acts.

And everything tastes like chicken,
   From rattlesnake meat to fried bats.
It has anonymous flavor;
   I figger they're all Democrats.

Some say this ignoble creature
   With his intellect unrefined
And lack of civilized manners
   Has little to offer mankind.

But let me suggest, the chicken
   Had two contributions to make;
The first was the peckin' order,
   The second, the chicken-fried steak!

Hey!
What about eggs?

On the Edge of Common Sense

By Baxter Black

Chicken Training

Illustration by
J.P. Rankin

SHE FELT an affection for chickens, she did,
    some might say it was overly so.
So when her good hens started showin' up dead
    it dealt her kind heart quite a blow.

The dog, she figgered, that pig-headed cur
    that helped the old man with his stock.
He acted like he was king of the place,
    the duly crowned cock of the walk.

She laid several traps and kept an eye peeled
    to catch the canine in the act.
She'd recently read in the *Poultryman's News*
    of a cure for these chicken attacks.

The method was crude but was flat guaranteed
    to put this behavior to bed.
At last she espied the ol' dog fast asleep,
    a chicken laid out by his head.

She put on a glove and crept out on the lawn,
    sneaked up and grasped the flat hen,
Then proceeded to wallop that fowl-killin' dog,
    with the chicken, I mean end to end!

JPRANKIN © 2000
"THE CARTOON COWBOY"

He dove for the doghouse, she followed him in,
    there ensued a bodacious uproar!
Timber and bedding and pieces of dog
    came boilin' out through the door!

Over the haystack and down through the creek
    and under the black silage tarp,
Leaving behind them a trail of yelping,
    of feathers, of dog hair, and carp.

She whacked him, she pelted, she thrashed him and more,
    till the chicken was threadbare and gray.
Exhausted she fell to her knees satisfied
    she'd applied the technique the right way.

She loosened her grip on the poor chicken's neck,
    a sacrifice made for the flock.
She laid the wee beast reverently out on the lawn
    and swooned when it sat up and squawked!

ON THE EDGE OF COMMON SENSE | BY BAXTER BLACK

MasterCard – Priceless

MasterCard has a very touching ad compaign they call "Priceless."

A dozen roses – $19.95
A diamond ring – $2,300
The answer "yes" – priceless

One of my friends is always on the lookout for an easy dollar. He suggested we think of some "priceless" ads that would appeal to the cowboy crowd. Then we could sell 'em to MasterCard and retire. Here's what we came up with:

A brand new super-cab dually with a three-horse slant – $54,650
2 trained Quarter Horses – $29,905
1 team-penning buckle – priceless

– or–

A 4-year-old registered
purebred Limousin cow – $4,500
Nine months feed and upkeep – $295
A healthy full-term bull calf sired by your neighbor's wanderin'
Corriente-holstein-cross named Elvis – priceless

– or–

A set of Crockett spurs – $139
A bull rope – $65
A broken arm – priceless

– or–

A successful Cesarean section on a mama cow – $190
A 110-pound healthy calf – $400
A missing pair of forceps – priceless

– or–

Complete set of horseshoing tools including anvil – $680
Book on how to shoe horses – $9.95
A horse who leaves tracks like the intersection of a drill
team's figure eight – priceless

– or–

A pair of Paul Bond boots – $600
A Bailey hat – $325
A 2 1/2-pound petrified wood bolo tie handmade
by your retired father-in-law – priceless

– or–

15 years of doing without,
working 12-hour days and reinvesting – $901,650
A ranch, a cowherd, a family – $3,650,720
An endangered mollusk discovered in the
one bog you left for the ducks – priceless

– or–

3 1/2 years of fun and playing around in college – $36,000
6 years of team roping, horse trading and farricry – $296
Marrying a woman with a good job
and a MasterCard – priceless